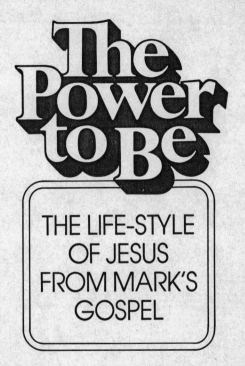

The Power to Be

THE LIFE-STYLE OF JESUS FROM MARK'S GOSPEL

Thomas H. Olbricht

JOURNEY BOOKS

An SPC Publication
Austin, Texas 78765

A complete *Teacher's Manual/Resource Kit* for use with this paperback is available from your religious bookstore or the publisher.

THE POWER TO BE

Edited by Ron Durham and Roger Hornbaker
Cover designed by Tom Williams

Printed in the U.S.A.
Library of Congress Catalog Card Number 79-67136
ISBN 0-8344-0108-8
5 4 3 2 1

Contents

...to Be UNIQUE 1

A man of twenty-eight sat in my office on Wednesday. He only recently had become a new brother. He grew up in a home without religious interests. In fact, at one point he considered himself an atheist. He had never read the Bible. On Tuesday night he started reading the Gospel of Mark. He got so involved he read it through nonstop. As he sat in my office he could hardly restrain his excitement. He had found the Gospel dramatic and compelling in a manner he had not anticipated.

My daughter was a student at the University of Indiana. One Saturday the Inter-Varsity Christian Fellowship on campus passed out copies of *Good News for Modern Man*, a New Testament translated and published by the American Bible Society. Several students around her dorm started reading in the Gospels, some for the first time. They were particularly intrigued by the Gospel of Mark.

Why are so many in our time finding the Jesus story, perhaps especially as told by Mark, so exciting? A new interest in Jesus is obvious. Jesus has become the focal point of plays and musicals. Books about him are found on the best-seller lists. Many well-known recording artists have produced songs which refer to him, if only cryptically. He has even been the subject of major television and motion picture productions. What forces have contributed to these emerging interests?

Jesus has aroused the interest of the computer expert, the college student, and the secretary because of his unique and definite manner of life. In our time many people have lost a sense of direction. They have forgotten or perhaps never known the ways of their ancestors. The older views no longer seem compelling. Identity crises are a commonplace human experience. Modes of dress have changed frequently and sometimes radically. New attitudes have emerged regarding material security and work habits. Certain legislatures have changed the laws on abortion and sexual relationships. Warfare has been examined from new perspectives, and unquestioning nationalism criticized. Many persons are casting about for new patterns of life. And Jesus has again come to the forefront because of his unique commitments.

In the midst of these upheavals, people of all sorts have looked for new models. In casting about to the left and right, up and down, we have struck upon Jesus. He has lunged forward to command our attention. He has an answer to the question of our times. We have asked, "What shall be my lifestyle?" We have found a new model in Jesus.

It is not surprising that persons searching for a

style of life have grown excited when they chanced upon Jesus. A fresh reading of his story when modes of existence are up for grabs has always had such an impact. The initial response to Mark's account was similar. The claims of this amazing man turned upside down an old civilization and laid the groundwork for a new one. The manner in which this Gospel infiltrated age-old Roman culture with a new life-style is intriguing.

A Unique Life

Why have persons in our time found the life-style of Jesus so impressive? It seems the leaders and authorities we know are so ineffective and powerless. Where is a leader today with a clear self identity? Where can we find someone who has declared who he is and what he is about, and who has stuck to that identity unwaveringly? One of the major problems of our times, apparently, is that leaders lack genuine credibility. We no longer demand purity of personal life. But we do hope for personal integrity, ethical commitment, and for courage, boldness, and compassion. And we have been disappointed so often!

Now turn from the present scene and take a new look at Jesus. What we have missed in persons of our time we find in him. He stands out as unique among all the important figures of history. He was different in so many ways we admire. One who reads the account of his life seriously has to be impressed with the courage, the discernment, the confidence, the credibility, and the compassion of this unassuming man. He was without authority or power bestowed by human governments or structures. He did not set out to be different just for the

7

sake of being so, but he was impressive simply because of the power of his being. He knew who he was, what he was out to do, how to get it done, and what the outcome of it all would be. The uniqueness of this man clearly lies in the fact that his life exhibited *the power to be!*

But we are likewise impressed by the fact that Jesus did not retain this power for himself. He drew close to a number of persons, both men and women. He walked with them and talked with them. He ate with them, he suffered with them, he rejoiced with them. They were an ordinary, non-committed, sometimes reticent, motley lot. But Jesus invested time and effort in a sharing relationship with them. And the outcome, after some months, is that he conferred upon them *the power to be!* And that is where each of us comes in. Jesus likewise confronts us as we take up his life's story. Through this channel we, too, are able to enter into a personal relationship with him. The outcome is that he likewise confers upon even us the *power to be!*

Transforming The Ordinary

Let us consider briefly a quite ordinary man whom Jesus met and eventually transformed by close association with him. The man was Simon, on whom Jesus conferred another name, Peter, that is "the rock" (Mark 3:16). When Jesus first met Peter he was a fisherman (1:16). Fishing was a respectable occupation but by no means a prestigious one. But Jesus was especially attracted to Peter. He was one of three who formed an inner circle of the twelve apostles. The twelve likewise were a more intimate group within a large band of persons who went about with Jesus.

8

In the early days what is most impressive about Peter is his eagerness. He was the one who acted (1:36) or spoke (8:29) first. He was a person of some courage but when challenged was quick to back down. We therefore conclude that Peter was impulsive. He was quick to identify with Jesus when the crowds shouted "Hosanna!" But toward the end, when everything went wrong and Jesus was taken prisoner, Peter denied that he even knew him. His denial was made to one who was not, after all, that important—she was only a servant girl of the high priest. "You also were with the Nazarene, Jesus," she said. But Peter denied it, saying, "I neither know nor understand what you mean." (14:67-68).

"But we also take up his story because of the hope that through knowing him we might become as he is."

In a few short months, however, a number of amazing events took place, and among them were changes which came over Peter. In the New Testament book of Acts, which tells the story of the deeds or acts of the close associates of Jesus after his death, Peter, like Jesus before him, is a person of power. We still recognize the earlier Peter, but there is a new style. He is bold and courageous (Acts 4:13). He is a man of commitment who sticks with it. He is decisive and confident. The change has come about because of his association with Jesus. Jesus has given even the impulsive fisherman Peter *the power to be!* And what Jesus conferred upon Peter has become the possession of countless thousands.

We, too, take up the account of the life of Jesus because he stands out in stark relief against a backdrop of bumbling, ineffective, contemporary leaders. He is unique among men. But we also take up his story because of the hope that through knowing him we might become as he is. It just may be that he will take hold of our weak, neurotic, uncertain, drifting existence and bestow upon us *the power to be!*

A Major Upheaval

It was about A.D. 27 when this man named Jesus attracted a large group of men and women because of his unique way of life. His early years were spent in Galilee, mostly around the sea. He lived and spoke as he did because he contended that God was about to break in upon history in a new and decisive manner. "The time is fulfilled," Jesus said, "and the kingdom of God is at hand; repent, and believe in the gospel" (Mark 1:35). Jesus made a tremendous impression in Galilee, then in other regions of Palestine, and finally in Jerusalem. People were struck by his authoritativeness and boldness. Yet as they watched they observed a compassion for people at all levels of society and perhaps especially for those at the fringes. He was confident, yet calm and unassuming. Those who knew him intimately were therefore shocked into silence when, at the insistence of the Jewish authorities, he was put to death by the Roman soldiers.

But an entirely unexpected turnabout happened. On Sunday morning following his death on Friday, Jesus' tomb was empty. Then he began to appear to people he had known. He showed up at gatherings of former friends in Jerusalem. He appeared to two as they walked along on a road outside the city. They did not recognize him at once. Later, one turned to the other and asked, "Did not our hearts burn within us while he talked to us on the road?" (Luke 24:32). Sometime later, Jesus showed up in Galilee and spoke to many who, dejected by his death, had returned there. As these men and women became acquainted with Jesus, they were still impressed with his person and lifestyle. But now they had an even more amazing story to tell. The one who taught with conviction, who healed with compassion, but who had been crucified, was alive again!

To this little band of old associates, Jesus' amazing return from death was headline news. They took aside friends and relatives and breathlessly related the amazing story. They repeated it hundreds of times to feast day visitors who had made the long pilgrimage to Jerusalem. They traveled from village to village in the countryside, announcing the good news along the paths, in the marketplaces, and in the quietness of thick-walled houses. The story was told thousands of times. We obtain some inkling of the manner in which it was presented from the early history set out in Acts. One sermon in particular seems to capture the essential points. It is the presentation made by Peter at the house of a Roman military captain named Cornelius, and found in Acts 10:34-48.

The Earliest Accounts

From the speeches in Acts we learn the basic outline of the Jesus story as first told. From these

11

speeches, presented by Luke in abstract form rather than in complete detail, we learn first that certain Old Testament quotations were considered to have reference to Jesus. These statements from the age-old Scriptures explained his unusual activities. As the tellers referred to the teaching of Jesus, or observed that he went about doing good, they repeated some of the examples over and over. They wanted to remember him exactly as he was. They told the story with attention to accuracy. Over the years these accounts were memorized by many because of the myriad times the same details were repeated. After some years, parts of the story were put into writing. Possibly a written account of Jesus' death was produced, as well as a collection of his sayings and the "signs" or miracles he performed.

As the years went by, those who had seen the risen Jesus traveled widely in the Roman Empire, telling the amazing news wherever they went. People were struck by Jesus' message and life—in Asia Minor, in Greece, in Egypt, in Italy, and in numerous other regions. Thirty years after the death of Jesus those who confessed that God raised him from the dead numbered more outside Palestine than within the very country where it all started.

Telling The Good News In Rome

Eventually those who walked the hills of Galilee with this astounding man found themselves farther and farther from their homeland. The original twelve apostles themselves traveled extensively. It is known that Mark, the author of our Gospel, spent some years in Rome. From 1 Peter we find a close connection between Peter and Mark. This connection is important for understanding Mark's Gospel. It may be, too, that Peter himself reached Rome.

At the end of 1 Peter is a statement which cryptically implies that Peter was in Rome when he wrote the letter. "She who is at Babylon, who is likewise chosen, sends you greetings; and so does my son Mark" (1 Pet.5:13). The word "Babylon" apparently is a cryptic reference to the city of Rome. The date of this letter would fall between A.D. 64 and 68 when Christians were suffering persecution under the Emperor Nero. The persecution was so severe that Peter did not dare openly identify the place from which his letter was written, since if it fell into the wrong hands further recriminations would obviously descend upon the Christians. (Further evidence that Peter was in Rome comes from Clement, a Roman Christian who wrote an epistle about A.D. 96 [1 Clement 5:4].)

When Mark decided to put into writing the story of Jesus, he was no doubt dependent to some extent upon Peter's memory of the Lord. It may, in fact, have been the death of Peter which spurred Mark to write the account. In that manner the story could be preserved and live continually in the hearts of new Roman brothers and sisters. The Gospel of Mark is therefore in essence, the "gospel of Peter" as told to Mark.

Added support for this conclusion comes from one Papias, Bishop of Hierapolis. Papias referred to the sayings of an elder he knew:

And the Elder said this also: "Mark, having become the interpreter of Peter, wrote down accurately whatever he remembered of the things said and done by the Lord, but not however in order." For neither did he hear the Lord, nor did he follow him, but afterwards, as I said, Peter, who adapted his teachings to the needs of his hearers, but not as though he were drawing up a connected account of the Lord's oracles. So then Mark made no mistake in this recording some things just as he remembered them. For he took forethought for one thing, not to omit any of the things that he had heard nor to state any of them falsely. (From *Exegesis of the Lord's Oracles*, now lost but quoted by Eusebius, the great fourth century church historian.)

Mark was a man of long association with those commited to Jesus. He had heard the story many times from those close to Jesus. He no doubt listened attentively as Peter repeated the story to various persons on different occasions. At some point he conceived a plan, in a sense unique, of putting the story in a written form. We do not know altogether what sparked this decision, though we believe that God himself was involved. But there were human developments too. It may have been the aging of Peter and the crisis of Roman persecution. Mark may have been spurred on by the death of Peter, as we have already suggested.

Sometime between 65 and 68 A.D. Peter was killed in Rome, according to certain later historical evidence. From the writing of a second century churchman named Origen, we learn that Peter was crucified upside down at his own request, since he felt unworthy to die like his master. Then it seems likely that two or three years later, or about A.D. 70, Mark put his Gospel in the final form in which we have it. He depended heavily upon Peter, as one can see if he compares an outline of the Gospel of Mark with Peter's sermon in Acts 10:34-48. But Mark also, no doubt, included insights from other Christian leaders with whom he associated.

The Roman Upheaval

We do not know whether the Gospel of Mark became an immediate best seller in Rome. But before long it apparently reached scribes, who produced multiple handwritten copies. These copies were first of all circulated among the Christians and their friends. How widely Mark's Gospel became known in Rome is uncertain. We do know, however, that from A.D 70. to 150 Christianity made tremendous strides in Rome. Apparently this Gospel made a contribution to church growth not only among the Jews who lived in Rome, but especially in the Gentile community.

Why did such widespread commitment for this carpenter, who grew up and died in far off Palestine, develop in cosmopolitan Rome? At this time, Rome was much like the same period 1,900 years later. Old life-styles were breaking up. The earlier Romans had been interested in practical affairs such as agriculture, commerce, primitive manufacturing, government, and conquest of other peoples. They emphasized traditional rules and laws in both their private and corporate life. But the winds of change were blowing in from the East. Rome had grown over the years and was no longer a country town of small gardens. People from the far reaches of the empire gravitated to her environs. They brought with them religions from distant lands, especially ecstatic eastern religions. The older practical and legal ways were being pushed into the background. The old heroes were disappearing. The government was unstable and frequently corrupt. The Roman historian Tacitus described this disconcerting situation:

> While things were in this state, while there was division in the Senate, resentment among the conquered, no real authority in the conquerors, and in the country at large no laws and no Emperor, Mucianus entered the capitol, and at once drew all power into his own hands.

> History 5.11

"He demands to supply power that we might be."

With all this breaking up of the old, with confusion at home and abroad, any ray of light shining through the darkness attracted attention. Soon, for many Romans, the figure of Jesus of Nazareth burned brightly across the blue Mediterranean and through the Truscan mountains. A new life model appeared. The authority and confidence, the compassion and humility of his life stood out. Here was the answer to the confusing, bewildering question of life style.

Now, 1,900 years later, the Gospel of Mark still has an electric message. We, too, have lost our way in the upheaval of traditions and folk mores. Jesus once again shines brightly in what he said and did, beckoning us to take up his ways. Once again he stands in bold contrast to the confused times in which people live. He beckons us at the very time in which the foundation of our existence seems threatened. He demands to be our model. He demands to supply power that we might be! Is it possible that once again he will turn a civilization upside down and take it for himself?

...to Be
UNASSUMING 2

Mark got right to the point when he addressed the Romans with the story of Jesus. He knew what sort of person Jesus was. He knew that the story, when presented straight-forwardly, would impress the Romans. And he was right! Mark may not have anticipated a time 2000 years later, but he no doubt believed that others would later read with enthusiasm of the unusual activities of the Galilean carpenter.

For Mark, Jesus was a most unusual person. He was a man who defied the ordinary. He commanded attention wherever he went. He stood out in the crowd. Mark could say, "Believe in him! If you are uncertain as to how to live, emulate him! In searching for a model, settle on him."

Mark recommended Jesus because he believed he was the Son of God (Mark 1:1). He knew others who, overwhelmed by what Jesus accomplished, confessed the same. He heard of the Roman army captain who stood awed as he gazed at the cross and the skies beyond. "And when the centurion, who stood facing him, saw that he thus breathed his last, he said, 'Truly this man was the Son of God' " (15:39). That should make a Roman sit up and take notice. If one of his own, and a hardened army captain at that, saw divine sonship in Jesus, he could not well dismiss it out of hand.

Mark indeed believed that Jesus was the Son of God. But that was not his first reason for relating the story. Rather he wished to declare what the implications of the Son's presence were. "Look," he was saying. "The Son of God lived upon earth for a time. He showed us, by what he did and said, how God would live if he became a human being. He set forth a model. He depicted the life-style God desires of man." And what was that life-style? Jesus spent his time with those who hurt. He usually could be found among the outcasts where suffering ran deep. He avoided the mighty and the powerful as regular companions. The key for understanding Jesus, according to Mark, was an alarming statement from the lips of Jesus himself: "For the Son of man also came not to be served but to serve, and to give his life as a ransom for many." (10:45). Jesus thus declared to those who followed him that the joy of life is found in serving. The way to life is the way of the cross. He commended that way to all comers. "If any man would come after me, let him deny himself and take up his cross and follow me" (8:34).

'Say Nothing To Any One'

Mark more than any other Gospel writer saw Jesus as having this unusual trait: he cared nothing for public relations. In fact, he worked to keep off the marquees and the front page. He had no desire to spread about what he had done, who he was, or his views on miscellaneous topics.

Mark begins with Jesus' early manhood and the start of his unique ministry. He tells nothing of his birth, of angels that sang, of shepherds leaving the fields, or wise men visiting from afar. Jesus went to the synagogue in Capernaum, the place where the Jews gathered for religious instruction. Though he did not readily identify with these people, on the other hand he did not shun being present at their gatherings. A man there had an unclean spirit, which upon seeing Jesus cried out, "I know who you are, the Holy One of God" (1:24). The demon confessed what men as yet were not prepared to affirm. Nevertheless, Jesus did not seek the acclaim. He charged the spirit, "Be silent and come out of him" (1:25).

"...His desire was to call attention to the work of God,...not to himself."

When the word of Jesus' unusual activities became known, many others came who were sick or possessed with demons. These demons wanted to publicly identify with Jesus. Again, Mark reports, "he would not permit the demons to speak, because they knew him" (1:34). The very next day as Jesus moved from town to town in Galilee, a leper approached and said, "If you will, you can make me clean" (1:40). Jesus was touched by the man, in his day a social outcast, and healed him. But Jesus did not wish this to become known either.

"See that you say nothing to any one; but go, show yourself to the priest" (1:44). Yet the news spread through the countryside like wildfire.

This strange lack of concern for fame was not just a feature of Jesus' early days of preaching and healing in the Galilean towns. Sometime later, possibly toward the end of the first year of Jesus' work, a synagogue ruler named Jairus came to Jesus because his daughter was critically ill. As most fathers, he wanted to do what he could. Her case seemed hopeless and he knew no place to turn but to this amazing, homeless Jew who had forsaken the carpenter shop. Jesus started home with Jairus. On the way a messenger met them with the news that the daughter had died. But Jesus was unperturbed. He said to the father, "Do not fear, only believe" (5:36). When they arrived at the house, Jesus said to those who mourned, "The child is not dead but sleeping." He then put everyone out except the father, mother, and three disciples. Taking the girl's hand he said to her, "Little girl, I say to you arise" (5:41). She stood up and they were all amazed. As before, Jesus wished no early morning headlines—"And he strictly charged them that no one should know this, and told them to give her something to eat" (5:43).

Despite Jesus' efforts to keep his action quiet, news often became known. When it did, Jesus wasted no effort trying to squelch it. Neither did he spend long hours devising strategy to completely cover up his tracks. But he tried to stay out of the limelight as much as possible. On one occasion he told a man, the demoniac healed in Gerasene, "Go home to your friends, and tell them how much the Lord has done for you" (5:19). But his desire was to call attention to the work of God, God's power over demons, not to himself.

The demons knew who Jesus was all along, to hear Mark tell it. Those who traveled with Jesus, the disciples did not understand. They saw him heal lepers and cast out demons. They heard his command to the storm, "Peace! Be still!" (4:39). They said to one another, "Who is this, that even wind and sea obey him?" But still they did not put two and two together. They were each one present when he fed the 5,000 (6:41-44), but the implication of it all failed to sink in.

Peter's Open Confession

Finally, however, the decisive day dawned. The light broke into their hearts. Jesus and the disciples walked toward the villages of Caesarea Philippi. On the way he asked them what people were saying. They reported that many were convinced of his greatness. Some thought he was John the Baptist come to life or one of the prophets. After hearing their report, Jesus put the question bluntly. "But who do you say I am?" By now they could no longer consider him a mere prophet. Peter answered, "You are the Christ." The word Peter used in Aramaic, the language he spoke, was *messiach* (see the English "messiah") which, along with its Greek equivalent *christus*, means "anointed." Among the Jews, the anointed one was king. David and Saul were anointed by Samuel, and Solomon by Nathan. In his confession, Peter expressed the weighty conviction that Jesus was the new king sent by God to introduce his rule, his empire, in a new and decisive way.

What a grand confession! But as soon as Peter

uttered the words, Jesus' aversion to fame arose again. One might think that Jesus would have planned for, anticipated, and longed for this day when his intimate companions would tell the whole world who he really was. Now they would spread the word. The headlines would blazon in bold type, JESUS OF NAZARETH IS MESSIAH! But Jesus had no such scheme—"And he charged them to tell no one about him" (8:30).

Six days after the astounding confession of Peter, Jesus took Peter, James, and John and withdrew from the press of the people. They climbed a high mountain. There, in an awesome series of events, Jesus was affirmed as Son by the Father. First his garments glistened, intensely white. Then Elijah and Moses appeared and talked with Jesus. And finally, a voice came out of a cloud, and said, "This is my beloved Son; listen to him" (9:7). What a great moment! What an impressive story to tell! But Jesus still desired no fanfare. "And as they were coming down the mountain, he charged them to tell no one what they had seen until the Son of man should have risen from the dead" (9:9).

Jesus likewise held no press conferences to make sure everyone knew precisely where he stood on the issues. Just as he wished no headlines for his actions, neither did he for what he said. Mark collected the parabolic teachings of Jesus all in one place (chapter 4). He first told the story from everyday experience of the man who went out to sow grain in his field. Some of the seed produced a crop and some did not. It was a simple story. It drew upon a life-related experience. The words were simple, but the point was not obvious. The disciples who had been with Jesus all along did not understand. "And when he was alone, those who were about him with the twelve asked him concerning the parables." Jesus' reply was strange, if not down right alarming. He did not declare, as do some, that parables after all are very simple since God wants everyone to understand. Rather, he responded, "To you has been given the secret of the kingdom of God, but for those outside everything is in parables" (4:11). He then explained the story. He also taught with other parables. Concerning these, Mark declared, "With many such parables he spoke the word to them, as they were able to hear it; he did not speak to them without a parable, but privately to his own disciples he explained everything (4:33-34).

Now all this restraint is a puzzle. Why did Jesus shun publicity? Why did he stop demons? Why did he command the healed individuals to remain quiet? Why did he speak darkly so as not to be understood except by his close associates? Mark gives particular emphasis to this personality trait of Jesus. Luke and Matthew speak of it, too. But Mark spends more time calling attention to it than the others. What point is he trying to make? If we can answer this question I believe we will have arrived at the profound meaning of the life of Jesus. We will have discovered the secret to what makes Jesus unique. At the moment this question may seem somewhat remote. You may ask, what all this has to do with the day-to-day routine of my life. But read on. The answer profoundly declares what a day-to-day following of Jesus entails.

Many Wrong Answers

The answers to this puzzle have been many. A traditional explanation is that Jesus shunned fame to avoid being declared a political king. He wanted to avoid, so it is claimed, the rule of a kingly hero after the fashion of Judas Maccabeus, a second century B.C. Jewish warrior leader who successfully revolted against the Seleucian empire, or of an earthly David or Solomon. It is true that John reports such concern in his gospel, "Perceiving then that they were about to come and take him by force to make him king, Jesus withdrew again to the hills by himself" (John 6:15). But John, in contrast with Mark, does not report the commands to silence. John further sets out a time schedule for Jesus, who must take care that his ministry does not climax prematurely (2:4; 7:6). For John, if Jesus is to do his Father's will he must stay out of the headlines. But despite scholars who have understood the charges to silence in Mark from the same perspective, Mark nowhere in his Gospel even hints that it is for this reason that Jesus pledges people to silence. In Mark, at least, an unfolding political timetable is *not* the reason for the hiddenness or the unassuming posture of Jesus.

It has also been suggested that his charges to secrecy showed Jesus to be a master strategist at public relations. Any psychologist can tell you that if you ask someone not to tell something they will soon have the news spread all over. It is human to want to tell a secret. It is true that the command to silence had this effect on the leper. He "went out and began to talk freely about it, and to spread the news, so that Jesus could no longer openly enter a town, but was out in the country; and people came to him from every quarter'' (1:45). But read Mark carefully and note that he never comments on how shrewd a psychologist Jesus was. He explains what happened when the leper broke the charge to show that Jesus' activities were so extraordinary that they became known despite his continued efforts to keep them under wraps. This psycholgical explanation may seem promising—but it is our suggestion, not Mark's!

"Rather, he came as Son of God to exhibit the very characteristics of God."

A German New Testament scholar, Wilhelm Wrede, called attention in 1901 to the secrecy motif in Mark. His own explanation has been largely rejected, but the importance of the motif has not been denied. Every scholar since has struggled with the so-called "messianic secret" and has come up with an explanation. Wrede claimed that the author of Mark (according to him not John Mark, but a later Christian) was embarrassed because Jesus did not openly and continually proclaim himself Messiah. If you read the Gospel of Mark, for example, you find only one place in which Jesus identified himself as Messiah, and even in that case he does so only when forced by a question from the high priest (14:61-62). The author of Mark therefore, wanting to offer some explanation, decided upon the device of Jesus' charges to secrecy as the reason he abstained from open Messianic affirmations. But it is not clear from the Gospel that Mark had any special interest

26

in the title "messiah." The term occurs in the Gospel only seven times, only half the number found in each of the other three Gospels. Mark was more interested in identifying Jesus as Son of God (1:1).

So the secrecy puzzle still eludes us. But the answer is actually simple. Mark highlighted the messianic secret to show that Jesus, the son of God, came not to dazzle people with an array of amazing feats and thus win fame far and wide. He was not concerned that people cater to him and respond to his every whim. Rather, he came as Son of God to exhibit the very characteristics of God—that he is a loving God, a God of great compassion and mercy. He is a God dedicated to helping his people. He is not like an Evel Knievel, seeking acclaim and hero worship through daring and extraordinary feats.

"...his life was not self-seeking, but dedicated to caring for and helping others."

Mark desired to establish what was true of the real Jesus, that his life was not self-seeking, but dedicated to caring for and helping others. He desired no acclaim. He wished only to serve. "For the Son of man also came not to be served but to serve, and to give his life as a ransom for many" (10:45). In both his life and in his death, Jesus showed the way of God among men. That way is the way of the cross, the way of service. Jesus not only gave his life as a ransom for many in his death. He *lived* for the same reason, not to benefit himself, but others. The life-style of Jesus shows that God, his father, is not interested in publicity

27

for publicity's sake. He does not cultivate the high and the mighty, but spreads his goodness among the sick, those who cry out in despair, the humble and the unassuming.

In one of the last statements of Jesus' teaching ministry, Mark makes it explicit that Jesus kept out of the headlines exactly because upstaging the other fellow is obnoxious to God.

> Because of the scribes, who like to go about in long robes, and to have salutations in the market places and the best seats in the synagogues and the places of honor at feasts, who devour widows' houses and for a pretense make long prayers. They will receive the great condemnation.
>
> Mark 12:38-40

Jesus came, not to be put on a pedestal as a hero or a miracle worker but to bring the compassion of God. He performed extraordinary feats, not to call attention to himself but to show man that God really loves him. Acts of love need no publicity. They are done for their own sake, not for some ulterior, hidden scheme of self promotion.

'Let Him Take Up His Cross'

So the power of Jesus' life came from what on the surface seems an upside down posture. How many people do you know who are in it for the other fellow rather than for themselves? How many people do you know who make it a rule to take care of Number 1, because after all, if you don't, who will?

The model set forth by Jesus is the opposite. He proposed that the way of life is not to first of all take care of oneself, but to care for others. "If any man would come after me, let him deny himself and take up his cross and follow me" (8:34). Then he gave the reason, a reason which at first glance seems contradictory. "For whoever would save his life will lose it; and whoever loses his life for my sake and the gospel's will save it" (8:35). Just what is this gospel, this good news for which one is to lose his life? It is that the secret of life is found in service to others! The gospel is about Jesus, and Jesus spent his life and his death for others.

The life-style of Jesus was the way of the cross. He commended the same path to all who seek the way of God in this world. With Jesus as our model, we have a concrete, day-by-day, hour-by-hour, life-style. Like him we shun the headlines. We look for ways to help others, not to get our names in the paper or to be seen on television.

"The life of the cross is not possible as a self-determined course. It is possible only because Jesus went that way first, then turned around and lifted us up."

In the church, the body of Christ, we seek ways of sharing with others in the body, not ways of being heralded in the church announcements or praised in the church bulletin. People who take the model of Jesus seriously do powerful works of love behind the scenes just as he did. They find life just as he did in the way of the cross.

The disciple of Jesus will be where he was, not in the blinding spotlight, not where it is always clean, respectable, and comfortable. He will be found at times among the outcasts, among the

29

dregs of society, where life is seamy, and dirt and filth rampant. It is possible for him to be there because he was exactly at the same place when God met him in Jesus. The life of the cross is not possible as a self-determined course. It is possible only because Jesus went that way first, then turned around and lifted us up. He likewise helps us to turn and lift up others. Even the twelve apostles did not understand immediately. After three years, they still envisioned following Jesus as securing for themselves prestige and privilege (10:37). Only later, when they realized Jesus trusted in God even into an unassuming if not disgraceful death, were they able to grant that life is to be lived God's way whether it leads to defeat or victory.

Amazingly, when we have taken up this way of life, what happened to Jesus also happens to us. In our efforts to shun acclaim, to stay in the shadows, we emerge. We become noticed, not because we seek it, but because the results of what we do cannot be hidden. We do not, however, let notoriety deter us from our set course. Jesus didn't. True, he became famous to many, and to others, such as the Pharisees, infamous. But he paid no attention. He kept his eyes and his hands focused on the work he came to do, to bring the compassion of God to man. "For the Son of Man also came not to be served but to serve, and to give his life as a ransom for many."

What a great model! What an amazing way of life! What a proclamation! The way to victory is the way of the humble. It results in both acclaim and defeat. But in the end time, the follower of Jesus, like his Master, will sit down at the right hand of God (16:19).

...to Be BOLD 3

Jesus is a classic study in contrasts and perhaps, to some, contradictions. He went in the other direction when he sensed a spotlight approaching. Such a person might appear withdrawn if not cowardly. He might appear to lack real drive. Apparently he was ready to settle for a private, mundane existence. Persons such as this we relegate to the corner while we search out those who relish the center of attention. We want to be where the action is. We want to get where the cameras are running. This Jesus, who sometimes seemed so reticent in a crowd, certainly would not command much of our time. We want to be around persons who come on strong; we want our models to be profiles of courage.

Known For His Courage

In spite of Jesus allergy to the spotlight, he was by no means timid. It is clear that Mark sees him as fearless against persons of all sorts and against dark and hidden powers. Despite his efforts to do his work behind the scenes, wherever Jesus happened to be, there was the action.

Once Jesus entered the country of the Gerasenes southeast of the Sea of Galilee. He was met by a man who lived in the cave-like burial tombs. The man was dangerous:

> He had often been bound with fetters and chains, but the chains he wrenched apart, and the fetters he broke in pieces; and no one had the strength to subdue him.
>
> Mark 5:4

Who could have blamed Jesus if he had retreated as rapidly as possible? Everyone else no doubt did. But Jesus stood his ground. He courageously faced the man with these extraordinary, demonic powers. He had no weapons, only the power of his word. But that was enough, and he commanded, "Come out of the man, you unclean spirit!"

Sought No Starring Role

Jesus sought no hero worship for his courageous deeds. That was not the reason he did them. He freed this man of those ominous powers so he could once again share life lovingly and meaningfully with relatives and friends. Jesus was not content with a weak and powerless existence. His life was bold. In fact it was a profile in courage.

Even Jesus' enemies recognized the strength and boldness of his character. They knew of his fearless posture in the face of terrifying pressure and power. They knew he didn't bow to anyone. He didn't, as a cowardly dog, tuck his tail between his legs and sneak out the back door at the appearance of acid-tongued critics.

> And they sent to him some of the Pharisees and some of the Herodians, to entrap him in his talk. And they came and said to him, "Teacher, we know that you are true, and care for no man; for you do not regard the position of men, but truly teach the way of God."

Mark 12:13-14

Word of Jesus' courage got out. There was nothing phony about it. It was not a front created by press releases and self-generated stories of amazing feats. It was for real. No calculated promotion was needed. A bold life cannot be hidden even by those wishing to remain incognito.

Jesus was known for his courage, not his recklessness. He did no daredevil stunts. He did not publicize amazing feats ahead of time to assure a crowd in advance. He did not jump from the pinnacle of the temple. He did not zap a boat out of the sea with a thunderbolt. He did not turn the high priest into an ape. If he was who Mark claimed he was, he could have done these and many more. But Jesus was not interested in fame and publicity. He was interested in spreading abroad the love and compassion of God to the humble and unfortunate. He faced demon-driven persons with courage. He confronted the power-driven officials who had forgotten about compassion. Even those who opposed him respected his boldness and single-minded devotion. Because of his courage, many believed in him, and followed him. They became bold as he was bold.

Jesus still inspires boldness in those who believe. We may sometimes have doubts, as did the first followers. We may sometimes move ahead cautiously, uncertain as to what action is demanded. But we know that bold deeds of love are required. Self-serving actions may create a stir but not a way of life by which one can live year in and year out. "For the Son of man came not to be served but to serve" (10:45).

The Ordinary Refused

There was nothing common about Jesus. At almost every turn he defied the ordinary. He confronted deteriorating powers of illness. He was aggressive against terrifying demonic forces. He assailed hunger, storm, and death. He stood his ground; he did not waver when attacked by influential religious figures. As Mark presents Jesus, his boldness unfolds in a number of different episodes.

Jesus, with his followers, was on his way from Galilee to Jerusalem. They went east of the Jordan, crossed the river, entered the city of Jericho, and then on the other side began the climb upward toward Jerusalem. A short distance out, a blind beggar named Bartimaeus heard about Jesus. When he perceived from approaching steps that Jesus drew near, he cried out, "Jesus, Son of David, have mercy on me!" (10:48). Bystanders tried to still the beggar, but he could not be silenced. They were either affronted or embarrassed by this no-good indigent. What right had he to make demands on Jesus? But neither his humble status nor his blindness irritated Jesus. He sent for the beggar and asked what he desired. The man replied, "Master, let me receive my sight." Jesus uttered simple words, but the results were astounding. "Go your way; your faith has made you well" (10:52). The crowd was obviously alienated by Bartimaeus. But opposing crowds did not intimidate Jesus. He did his acts of helpfulness regardless of what onlookers thought.

"But the mountain peak experiences in Jesus' ministry were few. He came to serve in the swamps where life is perilous, sometimes monotonous, and often meaningless."

Jesus went up a high mountain with Peter, James, and John. The three heard a voice from heaven declaring, "This is my beloved Son; listen to him" (9:7). God put his floodlight on Jesus. But there was no crowd present to witness this great occasion. He had brought only three persons along. It was a great mountain top experience for those present. But the mountain peak experiences in Jesus' ministry were few. That was not the point for which he came. He came to serve in the swamps where life is perilous, sometimes monotonous, and often meaningless.

"Come Out Of Him!"

So Jesus and the disciples came back down from the mountain. When the four arrived below, Jesus was confronted immediately with the ineffective and fumbling disciples. They, and now he, were challenged by a lad whose life was one affliction after another. This lad had a "dumb spirit," and his father had brought him to the disciples. The boy was continually tormented. "It seizes him, it dashes him down; and he foams and grinds his teeth and becomes rigid" (9:18). These demonic forces were too much for the disciples. The father told Jesus, "I asked your disciples to cast it out, and they were not able."

Jesus had given the disciples the power. He had demonstrated in their presence faith and courage in the face of evil. He was disturbed at their incompetence. "O faithless generation, how long am I to be with you? How long am I to bear with you? Bring him to me" (9:19). Jesus confronted the uncanny spirit with boldness. "You dumb and deaf spirit, I command you, come out of him, and never enter him again." It was a great victory! "After crying out and convulsing him terribly, it came out, and the boy was like a corpse."

Jesus did his work behind the scenes, sometimes for persons of authority and wealth, but often for the poor and outcast. He was no respecter of persons. He sought out neither the high and mighty nor the humble and lowly. He responded where people hurt, regardless of circumstances. But though Jesus worked as quietly as possible, he was by no means colorless and commonplace. He defied the ordinary.

Power Over Nature

Jesus was also dauntless in the face of natural forces, such as hunger. A large crowd met Jesus as he got off the boat on his way to an isolated place for retreat. His heart reached out to these ill and needy persons. So he disrupted plans to get away from it all. He had compassion and taught and healed. The hour grew late; the people became hungry. The disciples had a pedestrian suggestion—"This is a lonely place, and the hour is so late; send them away, to go into the country and villages round about and buy themselves something to eat" (6:36).

But Jesus was more audacious. "*You* give them something to eat," he said. So they discussed it, but their thinking was still bound by human consideration. They concluded that compared with such a crowd the amount of food they could buy would simply be ludicrous. But Jesus approached the absence of food with a boldness defying the imagination:

> And taking the five loaves and the two fish he looked up to heaven, and blessed, and broke the loaves, and gave them to the disciples to set before the people; and he divided the two fish among them all. And they all ate and were satisfied.
>
> Mark 6:41-42.

Jesus found himself surrounded by hunger. He called on powers from above and the hunger was satisfied.

On another occasion Jesus awoke to the lashing of the winds and the pounding of the sea on his boat. The disciples were out of their minds with fear. They felt powerless before these harsh forces of nature. Jesus was not alarmed.

> And he awoke and rebuked the wind, and said to the sea, "Peace! Be still!" And the wind ceased, and there was a great calm. He said to them, "Why are you afraid? Have you no faith?"
>
> Mark 4:39-40

No one, and no power, however ominous, frightened Jesus.

Affirming God

What was the source of Jesus power? How could he be so bold? We would like to know how Jesus felt about himself, and why. But Mark does not tell us. What he does tell us is that Jesus was affirmed by God. Jesus began his momentous ministry following his baptism, when a voice announced from heaven "Thou art my beloved Son; with thee I am well pleased" (1:11). We do not know how Jesus reacted to this affirmation. What Mark tells is that Jesus now went forth boldly and courageously to declare the breaking in of the kingdom of God and to fearlessly face the demons. Once again on the mountain, God vindicated and affirmed Jesus as Son. "This is my beloved Son; listen to him" (9:7). Because of that affirmation, he was able to heal the lad when the disciples had failed.

"Prayer is the affirming of God because in prayer we confess our dependence on him and our powerlessness apart from his power."

Jesus attributed his power to the fact that he in turn affirmed God. "This kind cannot be driven out by anything but prayer" (9:29). Prayer is the affirming of God, because in prayer we confess our dependence on him and our powerlessness apart from his power. Jesus was bold because he knew who he was. He was the Son so affirmed by the Father! He knew who was with him. He knew the capabilities of his Father. He saw no need for cowardice or for uncertainty. He was certainly not willing to settle for the customary or the everyday, even though he shunned whatever publicity his activities might bring.

Daring The Impossible

Jesus was not even beaten down by death. Jairus, a synagogue official, came to him as his daughter lay ill. Jesus started to go with him. On the way, a messenger arrived with news of the daughter's death. Even so, Jesus proceeded. A crowd of milling, wailing people stood before the house. They were lifeless and defeated.

Jesus said to them "Why do you make a tumult and weep? The child is not dead but sleeping." They could not believe their ears. Who is this dreamer? Who should be so audacious? "And they laughed at him" (5:39). But Jesus was imperturbed. He took the little girl by the hand. "Little girl, I say to you, arise." The words brought results beyond the parent's fondest dreams. "Immediately the girl got up and walked; for she was twelve years old." Jesus dared to do the impossible. Because he dared, it happened!"

Jesus was even so bold as to disregard his critics. His failure to be intimidated by Jewish officials was no small matter. They had authority and power. They could help Jesus get ahead, or they could impede him. Whether he lived or died was in their power. But Jesus did not worry about his reputation with them.

Soon they began to oppose him. They would see that if he did not dance to their tune, he would dance to none at all. Jesus went about his business of helping those who hurt. He didn't care what they thought. He did what God wanted him to do.

39

He was so bold as to march right into the center of their operations, where their authority was the greatest, and condemn what they justified.

> And he entered the temple and began to drive out those who sold and those who bought in the temple, and he overturned the tables of the money changers and the seats of those who sold pigeons; and he would not allow anyone to carry anything through the temple.
>
> Mark 11:15-16

The action of Jesus was not calculated to win friends and influence enemies. He was courageous simply because he believed his action to be the will of God. He no doubt foresaw the results: "And the chief priests and scribes heard it and sought a way to destroy him." But Jesus was bold because he believed God would in the end overrule evil men even if it required a resurrection.

'Have Faith In God'

"Jesus was courageous! But no human can be as bold as he. After all, Jesus was the Son of God." As humans, we rationalize this way. But Jesus did not. He called twelve men, and sent them out to challenge the powers which make men fearful. He gave them courage to face even the greatest obstacles. Just as he had been affirmed by God, so he affirmed the disciples. He expected that they, too, should defy the ordinary.

> And he called to him the twelve, and began to send them out two by two, and gave them authority over the unclean spirits . . . So they went out and preached that men should

repent. And they cast out many demons, and anointed with oil many that were sick and healed them.

Mark 6:7, 12-13

They were sometimes successful. On occasion they were ineffective. They obtained results when they depended on God. When they failed to look to him they fell on their faces. They clearly did not walk always on the mountain peaks. Jesus saw to it that they did the work of God by helping others, and not for self-serving or merely self-fulfilling reasons. When they failed it was for lack of courage and faith. This was the problem when Jesus and the three came down from the mountain and found the rest of the twelve defeated. Their weak faith and lack of courage left them impotent and withstood their efforts.

Jesus invited the disciples to live audaciously and courageously. Once he showed them it could be done by causing a fig tree to whither. He spoke to them of a life-style characterized by boldness and power:

> Jesus answered them, "have faith in God. Truly, I say to you, whoever says to this mountain, 'Be taken up and cast into the sea,' and does not doubt in his heart, but believes that what he says will come to pass, it will be done in him. Therefore I tell you, whatever you ask in prayer, believe that you receive it, and you will.

Mark 11:22-24

Jesus wants those who believe in him to be strong in faith. He wants them to be bold. He will give them the power. He will affirm them if only they will affirm him.

And when they bring you to trial and deliver you up, do not be anxious beforehand what you are to say; but say whatever is given you in that hour, for it is not you who speak, but the Holy Spirit.

Mark 13:11

Jesus gives the victory that God may be praised.

Our Own Boldness

We do not have all the powers of Jesus in our time. We do not have all the powers of the disciples. But because God is still with us, we do have power. Through his Son he has likewise affirmed even us. We should never underestimate the power of believing faith and prayer. Even we are asked to transcend commonplace, defeated existence. Even we are expected by our Lord to call upon him in order to defy the forces of evil.

"...God has not called us to resignation, but to boldness."

A man of twenty-eight with a wife and three children became ill. The symptoms looked bad. A surgeon explored the abdomen, discovered inoperable cancer in the lymphatic system (sarcoma carcinoma), and told him to contact his lawyer to make sure he had a good will. In the doctor's opinion the case was hopeless. The cancer had advanced and was so distributed through his system that chemotherapy was the only recourse. Most of those who heard the sad news were resigned to the inevitable. The cancer victim was sent to a hospital in Houston.

One man, a preacher and friend, stood by faith in the breech between his friend and death. He accompanied the man and his family to Houston. He counseled with him. He prayed with them, through long hours of the night. He suffered with him. In boldness, yet weakness, he stood by his side. Others despaired. He believed. He cried out to God. Sometimes, like the first disciples, his faith wavered. But he received new strength. He did not let up. He poured out his heart to God. And God heard, and affirmed the friend's sonship! The cancer is in remission. Hope abides.

What happened? A man of courage persisted in prayer. He claims no credit. He seeks no headlines. The only ones who know are those who have been informed by others. He simply believes that where men and women of faith are found, there sin, sickness, and death retreat into the shadows. He believes that God has not called us to resignation, but to boldness. He believes that God still calls those who are his to stand in the breech against failure and death. He believes it because we have been called to follow in the footsteps of Jesus. He was the bold one! Dare we follow him?

...to Be
OPEN 4

Great men are always busy. Jesus was no exception. He had a mission, a goal for his life. There was much to accomplish and only a few years to complete it. He knew how his days were to be spent. In respect to an hour-by-hour flow, his schedule was unscheduled. Jesus did not keep an appointment book in his tunic. His life, however, was a series of successive appointments—he simply turned the appointment book over to someone else. A statement from the Psalmist seems characteristic of the unfolding of Jesus' days.

But I trust in thee, O Lord,
  I say, "Thou art my God."
My times are in thy hand.

Psalm 31:14-15

The first action of Jesus after his baptism was Spirit-driven,—"The Spirit immediately drove him out into the wilderness" (Mark 1:12). On later occasions he re-entered the wilderness addressing God through prayer (1:35; 6:46). He took up his appointments as God assigned them, not according to some schedule he deemed crucial.

Our Hurried Schedules

We live hectic, sometimes frenzied lives. There never seems to be enough time. Committee assignments at church never seem quite finished. Lessons for classes go unread. Time planned for hospital visits erodes away. We promise to have people over for a meal, but time slips away. The latest books are begun, but they lie about with a marker at the end of chapter 2. Dresses remain unfinished on the cutting table. Unanswered letters stack up on the desk. The flowers need weeding; paint peels from the trim on the house and needs painting; a visit was promised but never made. There just isn't enough time.

Guilt sets in. Acid builds in the stomach. First one buys a roll of antacid tablets. They work for a time, but after a while we must have a stronger patent medicine. Next we need a prescription for pre-ulcer stomachs. Jesus had days like ours. He sometimes had to get away from it all. But he was never upset. He always faced the additional tasks calmly. He never complained, "there is just too much to do." Yet there was much more he could have done. He taught only a few of all the thousands in the small country where he lived. Most of the population of the world he neither saw nor touched. He healed only a few. He cast demons out only from those he encountered. He fed only a few of the hungry. Yet he always seemed to complete what he set out to accomplish. How did he do it? How could he be so relaxed under such great pressures?

'Before Day, He Rose'

Jesus had full days from the beginning of his ministry. As described by Mark, early on the first day of his teaching career he went to the synagogue. It was the sabbath (1:21). He was invited to teach and did so. He was confronted by a man with an evil spirit which he proceeded to cast out. As the day came to a close Jesus went to the house of Peter. There he was told that Peter's mother-in-law lay ill with the fever. He healed her and then ate (1:30-31). In the meantime, word of Jesus' healing power spread through the village and the countryside like wildfire. By sundown the sabbath was over and people could travel. They heard where Jesus was and came seeking him—sick people and those possessed with demons. They all gathered in front of Peter's house (1:32-33). There were so many Mark says "the whole city was gathered together about the door" (1:33). Jesus healed several. It was a long day.

"He accomplished what he could, and trusted his schedule to God."

But the next morning he was up early. "And in the morning, a great while before day, he rose and went out to a lonely place, and there he prayed" (1:35). As the rays of dawn broke the horizon, Jesus was away from people, alone with his father in prayer. Meanwhile, daylight was enveloping Peter's house, and the city was stirring again. Once again a crowd assembled and clamored for Jesus. Seeing he was gone, Peter and others went to find him. Finally, when they located him, Peter spoke out, half in reproach, "Every one is searching for you" (1:37).

Jesus did not reply, "Well, they can just wait. I simply can't face that mob right now." Neither did he complain about his exhausting schedule the day before. Yet, the schedule for the new day required him to be elsewhere. So he calmly said to Peter and the others, "Let us go on to the next towns, that I may preach there also; for that is why I came out" (1:38). He was not disconcerted over the fact that, while some demanded him in one place, duty called him to another. He had withdrawn to replenish his resources. Then, renewed, he set out to keep the appointments God had given him for that day. He fled no responsibility by not returning with Peter—in going to other cities he would face the same sort of crowds. But he understood that God's mission for him was to travel among the villages. He was not upset because that appointment prevented his doing what others would demand. He accomplished what he could and trusted his schedule to God.

He Committed His Appointments To God

As the days went by, more and more demands were made on Jesus' time. But he held up well. He did not collapse. He remained calm. After curing the man who lived in Gadara among the tombs, Jesus crossed in a boat back to Capernaum. The news of his return spread quickly. Soon a "great crowd gathered" (5:21). In the midst of all the excitement and the press of people, a synagogue ruler named Jairus worked his way through the crowd and fell at Jesus' feet. In despair he pleaded, "My little daughter is at the point of death. Come and lay your hands on her, so that she may be made well and live" (5:23).

Another might have been torn between going with the man and staying and helping all those who had waited so long. But not Jesus. Many requested his healing powers, but the case of the young girl seemed the most pressing. The others could wait. Should God will, there would still be time for them.

As Jesus started walking, a great crowd followed. One woman had a very pressing need. She had spent most of her livelihood on doctors trying to stop a flow of blood but with no success. Jesus seemed her only hope, and she could not let him get away. So she pushed through the crowd and touched Jesus. At that instant the hemorrhage ceased (5:29)! Jesus was doing his best to get to the house of the ill girl. But he perceived the healing power go out. He turned to the crowd and asked who touched him. The disciples demurred. After all, there were so many it could have been anyone. Furthermore, Jesus had no time to waste if he intended to get to the girl in time to save her life.

But the pause was worth it. "The woman, knowing what had been done to her, came in fear and trembling and fell down before him, and told him the whole story" (5:33). She did not know what to expect. Jesus did not rebuke her, or retort, "Look lady, can't you see I'm in a hurry? A little girl is dying, and I'm doing my best to get there!" We would have been torn at least three ways, but Jesus remained calm. He had a healing word for the woman. "Daughter, your faith has made you well; go in peace, and be healed of your disease" (5:34).

As he said these words, a messenger arrived with the news that the daughter had died. Jesus wasn't upset, though he certainly didn't exhibit a "who cares?" attitude. He avoided apologizing that there just hadn't been enough time. He spoke calmly to Jairus, "Do not fear, only believe" (5:36). Jesus was confident that if the Father willed there was yet time for the girl. And indeed there was! Through the power of his Father, "who gives life to the dead," he restored her.

Jesus took charge of events as they arrived, fully concentrating on each in turn. He did not become nervous over whether he had time to get everything done, hence destroying his effectiveness in the moment of action. He healed the woman in both mind and body by his words of compassion and power. He also raised the daughter. He did not "arrange his schedule." He let it unfold as it would. He committed his life, his time, his appointments to God.

And They Had No Leisure

The day arrived when Jesus sent the disciples out to put into practice what they had learned. They accomplished much. Like Jesus, they went out without appointment books, depending upon God to unfold the events of the day.

And he said to them, "Where you enter a house, stay there until you leave the place. And if any place will not receive you and they refuse to hear you, when you leave, shake off the dust that is on your feet for a testimony against them." So they went out and preached that men should repent.

Mark 6:10-12

When the tour was complete the disciples returned and gave a full report of all they had done and taught (6:30). Jesus recognized the pressure they had been under. So he said to them, "Come away by yourselves to a lonely place, and rest for a while" (6:31). They still had a heavy schedule. In fact, so many people pressed in upon them that "they had no leisure even to eat." They got into a boat and headed for a lonely spot where they could be by themselves. But the crowd wasn't put off that simply and noted the direction they headed. They started running on foot, collecting more people as they went. When Jesus and the disciples landed the same people were there to greet them—"As he landed he saw a great throng" (6:34).

"He relied on the flow of events because in them he found the hand of God."

What was Jesus to do? He could have said, "Now look—we are exhausted. We have made all the arrangements for a retreat. I'm sorry but you'll just have to wait. We're tired and in bad need of rest." Rather, "He had compassion on them, because they were like sheep without a shepherd, and he began to teach them many things" (6:34).

Jesus and the disciples remained on through the day teaching and healing. As night fell, large numbers still gathered. None had eaten unless they happened to have had a few morsels in their tunics. The disciples had food—five loaves of bread and two fishes. But what was that distributed to a multitude? Yet Jesus proceeded in confidence. He told the people to sit down in groups. Then he took the food. God had provided the day, the place, and the crowd. He would also provide the sustenance.

> And taking the five loaves and the two fish he looked up to heaven, and blessed, and broke the loaves, and gave them to the disciples to set before the people; and he divided the two fish among them all. And they ate and were satisfied. And they took up twelve baskets full of broken pieces and of the fish. And those who ate the loaves were five thousand men.
>
> Mark 6:41-44

Jesus' confidence, and calm, resided in the powers of the Father. If the Father determined the course of the day he could also provide the means to complete it as he willed. Jesus had broken his schedule. He had turned aside from a well-deserved rest because of the many in need. But he knew that another time would be available later. And it was! When the crowd had satisfied their hunger,

> Immediately he made his disciples get into the boat and go before him to the other side, to Bethsaida, while he dismissed the crowd. And after he had taken leave of them he went into the hills to pray.
>
> Mark 6:45-46

Jesus did not set up his schedule or worry over it. Yet he did not allow interruptions to control his attitude toward them. He relied on the flow of events because in them he found the hand of God.

51

Taking Time For Others

On several occasions Jesus interrupted what he was doing because of a request, though, as we have seen, not always. Once he was in Tyre, an ancient Phoenician city some fifty miles north of Jewish territory. "He entered a house, and would not have any one know it" (7:24). He was far from his own people, but he still felt the need for precautions if he was to obtain much needed rest. But the report of his powers preceded him even to this distant place. A Syrophoenician woman, more aggressive than the rest, came to Jesus and requested that he heal her daughter who was possessed by an unclean spirit. Jesus told her bluntly that his ministry was for his own people. But after more conversation he granted her wish: "You may go your way; the demon has left your daughter" (7:29).

On another occasion Jesus went to Bethsaida. Some people brought a blind friend to him, and begged Jesus to touch him. Jesus didn't complain about the interruption. He stopped what he was doing, took the blind man out of the village, spit on his eyes and laid his hand on him. The man would see again! What a happy group of friends that was! Jesus then returned to the disciples and proceeded to other villages (8:22-27).

Finally, the day came for Jesus to leave Galilee. He and his disciples started the journey toward Jerusalem. Whenever Jesus paused, the crowds gathered (10:1). On one occasion, as they stopped, the people brought little children for him to touch. Now the disciples were upset by these pushy, inconsiderate people. After all, Jesus' great accomplishments were too significant to be wasted just touching little children who, after all, are a picture of health. What a waste of time! Think of all the really sick people he could be healing! But Jesus rebuked the disciples: "Let the children come to me, do not hinder them: for to such belongs the kingdom of God" (10:14).

Jesus took things as they came. He did not fret about a disruptive schedule. Jesus' work was soon to end, but he did not fight interruptions. He could have pleaded with the Father, "There are just so many who need me. I have only been able to help a few. Can't you extend my great ministry?" Indeed, he accepted even the time of his death as an event scheduled by God, and as a fulfillment of his purpose.

> They went on from there and passed through Galilee, and he would not have any one know it; for he was teaching his disciples, saying to them, "The Son of man will be delivered into the hands of men, and they will kill him; and when he is killed, after three days he will rise."
>
> Mark 9:30-31

'Watch!'

In instructing the disciples, Jesus underlined the importance of turning over one's schedule to God. Man has to be alert and at work. He cannot sit around expecting an earthquake to move him. He must be alert, completing the tasks assigned. But while self-motivation is crucial, man can live in two ways. He can presume he has to get up, take the bull by the horns, and by sheer intelligence and studied judiciousness determine the future course of his life. He can get himself an appointment calendar and set out precisely how his days are to be filled.

But there is another way—the way of Jesus. This is, of course, to project goals and ministries, but to leave the day-by-day flow up to God. One works as energetically and as diligently as he can, but he does not lay claim to any completion dates. When interruptions arise they are accepted as God-given. Now, one faces each task as it appears, trusting its source as from God. He is confident that if God has given the task, he will also give the time to fulfill it. There is no lost motion. One can carry out the deed in calm confidence. He will not be so uptight that he bungles the task. He is relaxed. God has given the task; he will give the time to complete it.

"He is confident that if God has given the task, he will also give the time to fulfill it."

God determines the events on the headlines and on the calendar. He will bring it all to an end in his own good time. We need not face the end frantically. If you have turned over your appointment book to God, you will be able to achieve whatever God wants you to complete before life ends or history is consummated, whichever comes first. This is what Jesus has in mind when he tells the disciples to "watch." As history moves along, Jesus indicates that those who have put their trust in God need to be vigilant to complete his tasks for them as they arise. The disciples were sent out to declare the good news of the impending kingdom. They were told that "the gospel must first be preached to all nations" (13:10). There is much to do. The task is enormous. There will be no time to sit around.

> But of that day or that hour no one knows, not even the angels in heaven, nor the Son, but only the father. Take heed, watch; for you do not know when the time will come. It is like a man going on a journey, when he leaves home and puts his servants in charge, each with his work, and commands the doorkeeper to be on the watch."
>
> Mark 13:32-34

Watching means working—energetically, confidently, and meaningfully. It is to conceive each task completed as significant because it adds to God's plans for his universe. Even uncompleted tasks are exciting. They will be completed if God intends their completion. Of course, there are plenty of activities in the world which run counter to the designs of God. There is indeed a kingdom of darkness as well as a kingdom of light (9:42-50). But those who "watch" bring God's plans to fruition because they have turned over their life and their appointment book to him.

'My Times Are In Thy Hand'

We are astounded by Jesus' calm approach to scheduling. Almost everyone we know thinks if he is to get his share of the world's work done he must be a rigidly disciplined person. He needs to project a three- or four-year calendar, keep an appointment book, and maintain a rigid schedule. But it is well known that such a life-style takes its toll. Some days and schedules become hectic because of telephone calls and visitors. On other days equipment breaks and projects take longer than slated. Requests come unexpectedly. We hear this person's story and decide we cannot turn down so genuine a need. But we allow the interruption to disturb us because it has disturbed our schedule. After a time the pressure builds; we lose our composure; our disposition turns sour; we feel tension in our back; a headache comes on; our stomach starts to gnaw.

"If we were to accept the day and its flow of events as Jesus did, we could face it relaxed and with confidence."

But Jesus had all these pressures and more—yet he got more done! If we were to accept the day and its flow of events as Jesus did, we could face it relaxed and with confidence. Our attitude would be, "This is the day which the Lord has made; let us rejoice and be glad in it" (Ps. 118:24). Of course, there will be much to do. We have our work to take up, the ministry we have accepted, the tasks God has assigned. These may be regular and with prescribed hours. God is not simply found in the impromptu, the sudden, the unusual interruption. He is also in the recurring, the daily routine. He causes the sun to rise. He is a God who is faithful in promise, and relates to his universe in a scheduled way. His tides, his eclipses, his sunrise can be charted centuries in advance.

But he is also the God of the sudden storm, the different, the unusual. If there are interruptions in the course of the day, we accept them as God-given opportunities. When break-downs occur we do not become frantic. We either do the necessary repairs, or, if we must depend on others, we accept the work stoppage as a challenge to get on with something else. We do not know how we are going to get done all that needs doing. By just sitting and thinking about it and contemplating our own abilities it seems impossible that we can ever do it. But when we have turned our schedules over to God, we are confident he will give the time if he wants us to do it. Our moments and tasks then have real meaning because in them we do what he wants done. We face his day with joy and vigor. And when the day is through we bless God because he has helped us complete the tasks he intended for us that day. " 'Thou art my God' My times are in thy hand " (Ps. 31:15).

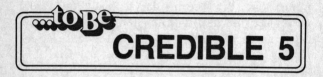

...to Be CREDIBLE 5

The Pharisees and Herodians put it to Jesus this way: "Teacher, we know that you are true, and care for no man; for you do not regard the position of men, but truly teach the way of God" (Mark 12:14). These words may be mere flattery. More likely, however, they are to put Jesus in an untenable position. Whatever the motives of these religious figures, as one reads Mark's presentation he is impressed with how these comments really capture an aspect of Jesus. The words ring true. Jesus was really that way. Jesus was his own person. He had credibility!

Unlike political types we know, Jesus did not seek the advice of his companions He did not authorize a public opinion poll to ascertain what position he should take on an issue. He did not sample Palestinian religious views or those of the Pharisees (or the brotherhood) to make sure he represented the mainstream. He didn't even consult friends and relatives for their opinions. Most of all he didn't become disoriented when the crowds went the other way, or when his friends charged that he was berserk, or when his disciples made wrong demands. Not that he was insensitive to people and only interested in himself and his projects. He was known for his love and concern for others, but not with respect to their self-serving desires and demands. He showed concern for men according to his own plans and ends. In a way, of course, they weren't *his* plans for he kept ever before him the demands of God. Jesus was his own man—under God.

Nothing To Hide

Jesus was his own person first of all because he withstood the powers of evil. He did not succumb to the enticements of Satan. Mark does not dwell on Jesus' confrontation with Satan. Matthew and Luke go into some detail about three temptations. Mark simply says, "he was in the wilderness forty days, tempted by Satan" (1:13). He was tempted, but resisted. He belonged to himself—not to alcohol, to sex, to ambition, to food, to an organization, nor to an evil power. He did not "carry a monkey on his back" as he walked about! However attractively Satan may have displayed his wares (and admittedly for most they have an overwhelming appeal), Jesus said, "No, thank you!" He did not sell his soul to the devil like Faustus, then approach the day when the devil would cash it in with enormous fear. The forces of evil had no hold over him. He continually withstood their bogus enticements. He did so because prior to his confrontation with Satan, God had affirmed him

Son. And that affirmation rang in his mind above all temptations.

Jesus had nothing to hide from God, from the powers of evil, or from man. Because he was tempted, yet resisted, he lived without fear that skeletons would be discovered in his closet. We know people whose lives are so entangled they live in constant fear of being found out. Some exhibit great ingenuity in hiding bottles and disguising their breath so the extent of their drinking will not be known. Others work out elaborate arrangements for meeting lovers on the sly. They live in such anxiety that they have prearranged signals in case a call is made at the wrong time or someone shows up at an inappropriate moment. These people aren't their own persons. They are enslaved to their vices. They live in constant fear of being found out. But Jesus did nothing of which he was ashamed. He had nothing to hide. No one held anything over him because they knew something he didn't want found out. He feared no man because his life was an open book. He was quite willing for anyone to know his thoughts or deeds.

He Was God's Man

Jesus was credible because he faithfully pursued self-determined goals. He was not one of those pathetic persons always worried about what someone might think. He did not expend lost motion carefully weighing means of guarding his influence. He maintained his integrity because he was not intimidated by his critics. He was intent on being God's man regardless of how his actions might look to others.

Early in his ministry Jesus came upon a tax collector named Levi. He asked Levi to be a disciple, and he obliged. Later, Jesus was eating with a group, probably friends invited by Levi, who were considered by the religious Jews "tax collectors and sinners." Such action could not fail but bring condemnation.

Tax collectors had a bad reputation for dishonesty and petty extortion. They were not paid a salary but bid for the office. They were required to turn over a set amount to the Roman government. Whatever was collected over and above that amount they put in their own pocket. Greedy tax collectors extorted from the populace as much as they could and were classified as sinners along with adulterers, robbers, and drunkards.

"Jesus showed himself to be his own man because he maintained his integrity in the face of critics."

Some of the scribes from among the Pharisees observed Jesus surrounded with these questionable persons. They had come, perhaps all the way from Jerusalem, to investigate first hand the unusual happenings in Galilee. "Why does he eat with tax collectors and sinners?" they wanted to know. Jesus did not say to himself, "Well, if respected religious persons think that way, I'd better get out of here fast. I will lose my influence if word gets around, and these people aren't worth losing my reputation." Jesus knew God loved even tax collectors and sinners. And he came to show the ways of God, not to win the accolades of men. So, Mark tells us, "When Jesus heard it, he said to them,

"Those who are well have no need of a physician, but those who are sick; I came not to call the righteous, but sinners" (2:17). Jesus showed himself to be his own man because he maintained his integrity in the face of critics. He did not permit them to determine where his God-given ministry was to be carried out.

The scribes and Pharisees were always kibitzing Jesus. Many a lesser person would have been deflated by their acid remarks. They would have left their ministry and taken up something else, such as selling lakeside cottages. If Jesus had been that way he would have retorted, "If they're going to stay on my back I'm going to go back to cabinet making. Being God's person isn't worth all that criticism." A person less sure of himself and less committed to his goals would have responded like a chameleon. He would have changed his colors at the remarks of the pointed-tongued critics. But not Jesus. In the words of Mark, "He cared for no man!"

'He Is Possessed!'

The scribes noticed Jesus' powers over the demons. They could hardly deny what everyone else observed—that demons did as he ordered. When he told the demons to move, they moved. Since the scribes could not deny his power, they sought to discredit it: "He is possessed by Beelzebul," they charged, "and by the prince of demons he casts out the demons" (3:22). These were respected religious leaders. By their own criteria and that of many looking on, they were good men. They stood with the traditional opinions of their Jewish brotherhood. But Jesus didn't flinch. He showed himself impervious to their devious ways. "He called them to him, and said to them in parables, 'How can Satan cast out Satan?' " These men were cruel. He was as religious as they. But he did not complain about their unfair tactics. He met the charge confidently and head-on. He did not attack the person of those making the accusation. He maintained his credibility to be just and loving, despite the underhanded attack by his opponents.

'He Is Beside Himself'

Some people are fearless when confronted by enemies, but give in to the desires of friends, associates, and relatives. They almost never refuse requests by those whom they admire. They want to be liked. They are too insecure to say no, for fear of damaging a relationship. But Jesus was not cowed by what friends thought. He even said no to the disciples when he considered their requests amiss.

Because of his astonishing feats Jesus grew so popular it even interfered with his eating. His friends thought he had gone too far. "And when his friends heard it, they went out to seize him, for they said, 'He is beside himself.' " (3:21). They were apparently embarrassed by his singular devotion to God. They were beginning to consider him what we would call a "religious fanatic." Some would say, "Well, if my friends think I am too involved, perhaps I should reconsider and take a second look." But not Jesus.

Not only were his friends embarrassed; Jesus' own family became concerned. We can hear a friend saying to James, one of Jesus' brothers, "Isn't your brother going a little too far?" James and his brothers finally decided he had gone far enough. "And his mother and brothers came; and standing outside they sent to him and called him" (3:31). For many of us that would have been it; we would have quit. Who wants to be at odds with his mother and his brothers? But Jesus stood up even under this pressure. He refused to depart at their beckoning. He did not belong to them. He belonged to God, and to whomever sought his way. "Here are my mother and my brother! Whoever does the will of God is my brother, and sister, and mother" (3:34-35). Jesus refused to let even those closest to him deter his being his own person.

But Your Disciples Do Not Fast

Jesus' public also made demands. Jesus attracted crowds but not because he worked at being a crowd pleaser. Some religious leaders are so conscious of their public image that neither they nor their families lead their own lives. The wife goes to the women's study group not because she really wants to, but because it will help her husband's position. The husband hates church business meetings, but he goes because he knows that only in this way can he be appointed to church office. The kids want to go to basketball games on Wednesday night, but the parents decide they have to go to church because otherwise the parents will be embarrassed at the questions of church friends. Now Jesus did not object to doing what religious people did. He regularly attended synagogue. But he did not do it to establish his image as a religious person. He was not motivated by what people thought. He did what he did to please God, not man.

Some even thought Jesus was not as religious as he should be. But Jesus wasn't disturbed. He believed his actions were acceptable to God. He was not worried if the religious types demurred.

> Now John's disciples and the Pharisees were fasting; and people came and said to him, "Why do John's disciples and the disciples of the Pharisees fast, but your disciples do not fast?"
>
> Mark 2:18

Jesus did not respond, "Well, I see what you mean. I guess people do expect fasting. I'm glad you pointed it out to me." He calmly raised a question of the critics. "Can the wedding guests fast while the bridegroom is with them?" Jesus was not religious enough for some, and too religious for others. But he did not permit the opinion makers to sidetrack him from what he understood as his God-given mission.

"Jesus did not belong to the crowds. He belonged to God."

There were times when Jesus failed to make a social appearance when demanded. He was never the sort who said, "Well, I have to go—my public is calling." Not that he was self-centered or had a prima donna complex. He responded to Roman army captains, to beggars and lepers, to Pharisees and rich tax collectors. He even interrupted his vacations to help others (6:30-34). But Jesus did not cast himself in the role of crowd pleaser. He preferred to be a God pleaser—to fulfill the ministry God gave him.

> And in the morning, a great while before day, he rose and went out to a lonely place, and there he prayed. And Simon and those who were with him followed him, and they found him and said to him, "Every one is searching for you." And he said to them, "Let us go on to the next towns, that I may preach there also; for that is why I came out."
>
> Mark 1:35-38

From all we know Jesus did not even dress just to please people. He did not wear his hair a certain way to cater to either the young or the old. If he did, no one considered it significant enough to record. And as far as we can tell he did not continually worry about and refine his way of preaching. Jesus did not belong to the crowds. He belonged to God.

'Do For Us Whatever We Ask'

Even Jesus' students, his disciples, did not sidetrack him from what he saw as right and necessary. Some students twist their teachers around their little fingers. These are teachers who desire acceptance. Jesus was not that kind of a teacher. Even his favorite disciples failed to wheedle special privileges of a self-serving sort. When Jesus went to the mountain he took Peter, James and John. It is clear they were his favorites. They were awed with what they saw on the mountain. They began to get the message that Jesus had a special relationship with God. They wanted in on the action. "Teacher, we want you to do for us whatever we ask of you" (10:35). They apparently thought

66

they had it made. But Jesus didn't accomodate them. He might lose a disciple or two, but so be it! "To sit at my right hand or at my left is not mine to grant, but it is for those for whom it has been prepared" (10:40). Jesus was openly critical of the disciples when they needed it, as for example, when they tried to keep away little children:

And they were bringing children to him that he might touch them; and the disciples rebuked them. But when Jesus saw it he was indignant, and said to them, "Let the children come to me, do not hinder them."

Mark 10:13-14

Jesus did not play favorites, even with those he liked best. He was sensitive to people but for God's reasons.

'You Will Be Hated By All'

Not only was Jesus his own man under God, he expected his disciples to follow suit. He sent them out and charged them to be dependent on no one thing, or anyone, except God alone.

He charged them to take nothing for their journey except a staff; no bread, no bag, no money in their belts; but to wear sandals and not put on two tunics. And he said to them, "Where you enter a house, stay there until you leave the place. And if any place will not receive you and they refuse to hear you, when you leave, shake off the dust that is on your feet for a testimony against them."

Mark 6:8-11

Like Jesus, the disciples would be criticized by both friends and relatives. But Jesus withstood the pressures, and they were expected to withstand.

> And brother will deliver up brother to death, and the father his child, and children will rise against parents and have them put to death; and you will be hated by all for my name's sake. But he who endures to the end will be saved.
>
> Mark 13:12-13

At first Peter did not hold up. He succumbed to the opinions of others. Jesus predicted Peter's weakening. He told him that before the cock crowed twice Peter would deny him three times (14:30). Peter was upset. He would never deny his Lord! But he did not calculate how strong the forces of public opinion are. On that occasion Peter turned out not to be his own man!

> And after a little while again the bystanders said to Peter, "Certainly you are one of them; for you are a Galilean." But he began to swear, "I do not know this man of whom you speak."
>
> Mark 14:70, 71

Peter stumbled. Jesus knew that God called man to perfection just as he himself is perfect. But he was also aware that man often falls short. Peter could still emerge as his own person, in spite of his downfall. He could do so because God forgives and loves again freely. After the resurrection Peter was particularly affirmed when the angel said, "Go, tell his disciples and Peter that he is going before you to Galilee; there you will see him" (16:7).

Joseph of Arimathea, a follower but not a close disciple, turned out opposite from Peter. Joseph had much to lose since he was "a respected member of the council" (15:43), the country's ruling Jewish body. The decision of Joseph's colleagues was against Jesus. But Joseph took his stand, even at the possible loss of income. He had become impressed with Jesus, and had learned not to be intimidated by the opinions of men. He, therefore, "took courage and went to Pilate, and asked for the body of Jesus" (15:43). Joseph proved to be his own man. He re-enacted the life-style of Jesus.

Being God's Person

By his credibility Jesus commends to us a new way of life. By his resistence to evil he says to us that we need not live under the weight of guilt and sin. We need not be overawed by those who threaten to expose us for our heterodoxies. We need not live in fear that our friends might turn their backs on us. We need not succumb to undue pressure from the opposition of close relatives. We need not be intimidated by popularity, or lack of it, with individuals, crowds, or students. We can turn our back on all these pressures and be our own person. Jesus did it, and he gave us power to do the same. But then, it's not really to be our own person, but God's woman or God's man.

...to Be
DISCERNING 6

In periods in which traditional ways of life are coming in for criticism, Jesus is frequently heralded as hero of the revolutionaries. In the early 1960's from several quarters long-standing rules and life-styles began to be held up for closer scrutiny. Near the end of that decade, groups reacting against traditional ways began to break out everywhere, especially in America. Among some groups during this period Jesus came to the center of the stage. This was the time of the short-lived "Jesus movement."

The interests in Jesus were various. The "Jesus people" were conservative in theology but radical in appearance. They wore long hair, beards, and older country-style clothes. They formed commune-like compounds even though they distinguished their groups from those which left traditional moral restraints. But various others, tired of church-going suburban communities of the 1950s, reacted with considerable violence. Some even came out against law and order, making a textbook of Henry Thoreau's writings on civil disobedience. Revolution was in the air. It is therefore not surprising that certain scholars and popular writers, hoping to capitalize on these new interests, began publishing books proclaiming Jesus as "the Revolutionary."

There is, of course, a great truth in this title for Jesus. But as with so many fads the question was not raised often enough whether the revolution Jesus initiated was anything like that of the '70s. One does not identify with Jesus simply by being a revolutionary. Rather one must be revolutionary for the same goals and reasons. Jesus is not the progenitor of revolutionaries of all stripes and colors; only those who seek to turn upside down civilizations for the new and unique ways of the kingdom of God.

There was, admittedly, a revolutionary difference in Jesus. He did not exactly square with typical folkways of his time or any time. Where Jesus is taken seriously upheavals have always occured, beginning with the Empire of Rome in the first century. This often happens even today among those who take a strong look at Jesus for the first time. Jesus creates revolutions. But his revolutions are seldom those of past western history—for example, the French, the Chinese, the Communist, or even the American Revolution. Nor does it seem that any present revolution can claim Jesus completely in respect to methods and programs. Particularly in attitudes towards laws, traditions, and rules, Jesus was on a different wave length. He did little to challenge or break laws. He abided by most of the customs. It was primarily his actions within the framework of law and order that he disturbed people. He burned no buildings, led no protest marches, staged no sit-ins before administrative offices, took over no buildings, nor master-minded any mass demonstrations. He called for a number of revisions. But it was what he did within the existing orders which gave his life a revolutionary flavor.

Jesus did not come off as a law breaker or an inveterate opponent of rules. But he did identify a number of wrongs which needed to be made right. And he proposed a new and revolutionary manner of life. What was the style of Jesus in respect to laws and rules? The answer is multifold. Let's look at the facts.

He Entered The Synagogue

We read of Jesus teaching at lakesides. We are told he healed along the roads on which he traveled. He spoke in village streets, in the houses of common people, in the field, and on the hillsides. Thus we might conclude that the activities in which he engaged were all beyond the confines of organized religion. We might even depict him as anti-establishment. We might see him throwing about such mottos as "God yes, the synagogue no!" Or "God turns me on, the synagogue turns me off!" Such a conclusion, while having some substance, is too hasty.

Jesus carried on his ministry everywhere, including within the structure of established religion, and with religious leaders and people. He did not identify too readily with the leaders of the Jewish religious establishment. But his conflicts with their positions did not preclude his appearing and speaking at the official religious gatherings. Apparently he was regular in attendance at the synagogue. He frequently spoke at the invitation of the synagogue rulers. Obviously, they did not all approve of him, but they did not bar him from participation. Jesus knew that many took a dim view of his actions and ideas, but he did not drop out. He carried on his ministry within the confines of law and order and religious traditions. Jesus sometimes met with close friends in houses, but these meetings did not take the place of synagogue attendance. The synagogue had a president, a man who made arrangements and gave direction. But there were no official teachers or preachers for each synagogue. Any male present who so desired was permitted to speak, at least as long as the comments over a period of time did not undercut the views and authority of the synagogue. It was partly because of this fluid teaching arrangement that Jesus could work within the system.

The first time Mark tells of Jesus speaking to a crowd is in the synagogue of Capernaum. It was the sabbath (1:21). On that particular occasion he was well received. "And they were astonished at his teaching, for he taught them as one who had authority" (1:22). In fact, because of what happened at the synagogue "his fame spread everywhere throughout all the surrounding region of Galilee" (1:28). Shortly afterwards Jesus took a tour of a number of cities and likewise preached in their synagogues (1:39). At least at this stage, the assemblies of organized religion were his arena of operation.

After a time, however, certain actions of Jesus

brought criticism from the religious leaders. One sabbath Jesus was going through the grainfield with his disciples. As they made their way, the disciples pulled off heads of grain and ate it. Certain religious traditionalists were in the group. They blurted out, "Lord, why are they doing what is not lawful on the sabbath?" (2:24). Jesus came to their defense. He pointed out that according to the Scripture, David, whom they revered, entered the tabernacle once when he was hungry and ate bread which only priests could lawfully eat. And not only did he eat it himself, but he gave it to those who were with him. Then Jesus uttered a discerning conclusion: "The sabbath was made for man, not man for the sabbath; so the Son of man is Lord even of the sabbath" (2:27-28).

The Pharisees' legalistic interpretation of the sabbath was wrong. It hindered man rather than helped him. According to Jesus, that was not God's intent. The sabbath was given to provide man a day of rest, not to prevent him from eating, if hungry. The way of the Pharisees is similar to the objection to blood transfusions on the ground that the Christian is prohibited from eating blood (Acts 15:29). Such interpretations apply rules where not intended, and to the hurt rather than help of human beings.

But even this criticism did not alienate Jesus from the synagogue. Mark makes it a point to declare that Jesus continued frequenting the Jewish gatherings for teaching and worship. "Again he entered the synagogue" (3:1). Jesus certainly was not a revolutionary in terms of breaking up the times and places where religious persons met.

It is important to notice that the synagogue, with

its rules, was a religious custom. Neither such gatherings or synagogue procedures are to be found in the Old Testament. Synagogues came on the scene about the time the Old Testament was completed—that is, about 400 B.C. Jesus never criticized the synagogue as an institution, despite the fact it was not authorized by the Old Testament. Even when Jesus returned to his hometown, and despite their indifferences and sacrasm, if not down right rejection, he still attended the synagogue gathering and spoke (6:2).

A House Of Prayer

Mark reports only one trip of Jesus to Jerusalem. We are not told by Mark, or the other Gospel writers for that matter, whether Jesus worshiped at the temple according to the law. But apparently Mark wished to leave that impression. Upon arriving in Jerusalem, Jesus headed straight for the temple. "And he entered Jerusalem, and went into the temple" (11:11). What he did there we are not told. Some believe he went through the usual cleansing ceremony. He did if he desired to worship in the official manner. Jesus didn't have much time for all the arrangements on the first day. He spent the night in Bethany and returned the second day. It seems likely that on the second day he fulfilled the requirements of the law if he did so at all. Later that day Jesus drove out the Jews who sold and bought in the temple (11:15). His action in this case was definitely anti-establishment. The Jewish leaders interpreted it in that way. But Jesus' action was not against the temple. It was against the manner in which the temple was being used: "Is it not written, 'My house shall be called a house of prayer for all the nations? But you have made it a den of robbers.' '' (11:17)

Such action might be taken as the dramatic protest of a revolutionary. But Jesus intended it rather as a way of pointing to the age-old plans of God. He sought to return the temple to the use declared in the Old Testament. But one should also note in the quote that the temple as a place of prayer was not just for the Jews but for the *nations*. Jesus believed that God was now at work completing his promises from of old that all men would worship him together. The Jews would be included but only if they were willing to receive all nations as God had promised from time immemorial.

Jesus returned to the temple on the third day (11:27). We are not told what he did, but as he was leaving the priests, scribes, and elders engaged him in conversation. Just as in Galilee Jesus taught in the synagogue, so in Jerusalem he taught at the temple (12:35; 13:1). While in Jerusalem Jesus and the disciples also kept the passover in the traditional manner. They made all the necessary arrangements on the first day of Unleavened Bread for sacrificing the passover lamb (14:12-25). Apparently all his life Jesus made it a practice to keep the passover according to the law.

In respect to rules and customs Jesus looked essentially like any other good Jew. He would not have been asked to speak in the synagogue had that not been the case. Jesus was not out to break the molds. What Jesus did and said did irritate the religious leaders but not because he opposed law and order. If one accepted their principles of interpreting Scripture, the Jews were right. But Jesus considered their method of interpretation narrow and limited. Jesus believed the Scriptures pointed to more exciting horizons. As Son of God the prerogatives certainly rested with him. The problem was, the Jewish leaders did not accept his Sonship.

Giving Caesar His Due

Jesus not only upheld the law and customs of the Jews, but also those of the Roman overlords. There is the famous story of the Pharisees asking Jesus whether a Jew should pay the Roman tax. The Pharisees carefully planned the question as a trap. If Jesus said yes, he would certainly lose popularity with the crowds.

"Jesus saw no point in changing such structure apart from changing first the hearts of men."

Most people, then and now, do not relish paying taxes. The Jews found the Roman taxes even more odious for they were paid not to their own government but to their conquerors, the uncircumcised Romans. If Jesus said no, he would win friends among the populace. The Pharisees likely expected him to say no, for they no doubt saw him as a man on an ego trip who had achieved his success by playing to the stands. But if he said no, the Pharisees had him where they wanted him. They could go immediately to the Roman officials. Such a view expressed openly would constitute sedition. The Jews would not need to contrive further charges to silence Jesus. The Romans would take care of it.

But Jesus did not see the tax as a big matter. He shared neither the Pharisees' nor the populace's interest in the matter. His concern was for the ways of God. He simply responded, after requesting a Roman coin, "Render to Caesar the things that are Caesar's and to God the things that are God's" (12:17). Jesus was quite content to live within the established economic and political boundaries. His chief concern was a single-hearted devotion to God. If men and women dedicated to God changed economics and government to reflect their God commitment, fine. But Jesus saw no point in changing such structures apart from changing first the hearts of men.

'You Leave The Commandment Of God'

Though Jesus lived within the framework of societal rules, he did not support without question all religions and customs of the time. he certainly did not seek out public opinion and champion the status quo. Some people make their mark in life by becoming a public spokesman for what the majority stands for, and opposing what they oppose. But not Jesus. Some of the customs he ignored. Others he kept. If criticized for departures, he gave his reasons.

There was the grainfield episode. Some of the disciples pulled grain and ate. Certain Pharisees were in the entourage and objected. Jesus considered their objection obtrusive (2:25-26), but he did not propose that the sabbath law be abolished. He had no bad word for the law. He said it should not be interpreted so as to violate its intent. Apparently, in the view of Jesus, the letter of the law is not what comes first, but the law's intention. We need to be clear that Jesus was not against law. He was not a libertine—that is, one who thinks a person should do what feels good. Neither was he an antinomian—that is, one against law from some philosophical position, usually that man truly becomes man when he follows the dictates of nature or of love rather than law. For Jesus, in order to determine how the law is to be applied, one must understand its intentions. And the intentions of God's law are for the good of man, not to his harm.

"The sabbath rules weren't for inhibiting man, but for helping him."

What then was the intent of the sabbath law? Jesus declared, "The sabbath was made for man, not man for the sabbath" (2:27). Actually, Jesus did not coin this phrase. It was around among the rabbi's. But the phrase represented Jesus' point of view. God did not first create the sabbath as being good in itself, then think up some being, for example man, who would benefit by observing it. God created man first of all; then in considering his wellbeing, he gave him the sabbath. Continuous work without rest is harmful to man. The sabbath rules weren't for inhibiting man but for helping him.

Some persons actually seem to picture God as a motorcycle policeman hiding behind a billboard to catch the unsuspecting. They see God as just sitting around waiting to nab the rule-breaker. He takes great delight in exclaiming, "Ah-hah! I caught you this time!" Similarly, the Pharisees saw the law as obviously more important than man. In their worst moments, they even saw the law as prior to God himself. When it came to the law even God's hands were tied. But that was not the way Jesus saw it, nor for that matter the Old Testament itself. From the perspective of the Old Testament the law was created by God, and it was his prerogative to do with it as he pleased. He was not subject to his law. Should it serve his purpose, he was willing to wave the law, as he did in the case of the people who hoped to worship at the temple from the north in the days of Hezekiah. (See 2 Chron. 30:10-22.) Of course, for the most part the law stands since God above all is faithful, and laws have to do with faithfulness, both on the part of those who keep them and God who promises blessing for laws kept. So the sabbath law was good, but not a letter-of-the-law interpretation of it, according to Jesus.

But Mark wished to make another point. Jesus is the Son of man, the One sent from God to establish the kingdom of God as a representative of man (Dan. 7:13-14). The law was created by God, and it is therefore the prerogative of the Son to interpret the law of the sabbath, since he is its Lord.

Right after the grain field incident Jesus was accused of another sabbath violation. A man with a withered hand entered the synagogue (3:1). The Pharisees watched like hawks to see what Jesus would do. He asked a question: "Is it lawful on the sabbath to do good or to do harm, to save life or to kill?" The man with the withered hand was not in any immediate danger, but restoration to ordinary usage would be a great boon. It would do more for him than a day of rest. Jesus restored the hand.

The Pharisees couldn't do anything just then, but they were writing it all down. This was another violation. "The Pharisees went out, and immediately held counsel with the Herodians against him, how to destroy him" (3:6). The matter was something like the question of whether one should seek employment in a hospital since one will have to work on Sunday during worship services.

Responding To Rules And Regulations

The Pharisees watched Jesus incessantly. They were ready to add to his list of infractions anything halfway qualifying. They noticed that some of the disciples did not wash their hands before eating. Jesus was not against such traditions. We have seen that in the case of the synagogue traditions. But he was against making too much of them, especially trying to bind them on people as the rules of God. It is especially sad, he said, when we think more of the traditions of men than the commandments of God. "You leave the commandment of God, and hold fast the tradition of men" (7:8).

But people sometimes get caught up in strange controversies. It was a sad day, for example, when modern traditions concerning hair length and style became more important than whether one helped his neighbors in time of need. The Pharisees even created some traditions which circumvented the commands of God. Jesus understood the commandment to "Honor your father and your mother" (7:10) to include helping them financially in old age, if necessary. But traditions had built up whereby if one dedicated property or goods to God he could continue to control it. He could not, however, use it to support his parents since, as the tradition was understood, that would involve giving to the parents what belonged to God. If his needy parents made a request, he could simply reply "It is Corban" that is, a gift (7:11). That was the same as saying that his hands were tied; he had no responsibility. But all this was a tradition, not the intent of the law of God.

Finally, in this incident, Jesus dealt with the Jewish tradition about hand washing. He said there is something worse than unclean hands, namely an unclean heart. The defilement one takes in through his mouth from unclean hands is not nearly so damaging as what a man does, says, and thinks when his heart is unclean.

"When he opposed rules, it was not the rules per se, but their interpretation."

Jesus' comments on divorce show that he certainly was not revolutionary in that respect, if by revolutionary one means a preference for a society without rules. On divorce Jesus was more rigid than commonly accepted Jewish customs. He asserted that God did not actually favor the turn taken by the Jewish divorce laws. "Whoever divorces his wife and marries another, commits adultery with her" (10:11). The law of Moses permitted divorce. Jesus said that God granted such a relaxing of the rules because of the hardness of people's hearts. He apparently had in mind that they were stiffnecked people, always preferring what they wanted rather than what God wanted (10:5). God is not so inflexible that he cannot be moved by human wants. But he continually tries to bring those made in his image to his ways. His ways are the right ways because he has made everything, and he, more than anyone else, knows how it should be so as to turn out right.

In his word and action, his life-style, Jesus shows a discerning responsiveness to rules and regulations. When he opposed rules, it was not the rules per se, but their interpretation. If rules are construed to deprive the hungry, the malformed, the needy, then he saw the interpretation as wrong. Otherwise, Jesus encouraged his disciples to keep the rules and laws.

Discerning Rules' Intent Today

We, too, should follow Jesus by living within present structures and traditions. We have seen that Jesus taught this to his disciples in respect to paying the government tax. That does not mean that we keep the laws simply because they are there and always uphold standard interpretations. We, too, if we follow Jesus, must be sensitive to misapplied rules. For examples, Paul once wrote, "So then, as we have opportunity, let us do good to all men, and especially to those who are of the household of faith" (Gal. 6:10). It would be a strange outcome to insist that this means the church cannot help the needy non-Christian, as has sometimes been argued. Jesus himself certainly helped non-Jews (7:28). What Paul apparently had in mind was that we cannot help every needy person. We should help as many as we can and especially those who are brothers and sisters in Jesus. The good Samaritan who helped the man in need even though a stranger and of another religion is the ideal. He helped him because there, concretely before his eyes, was a person in genuine need. The Samaritan man didn't set up a program for assisting all those robbed, and Jesus did not condemn him for his failure to do so. But he helped the injured man without regard for anything but his need.

Once some Christians in the Midwest decided to start a children's home to care for parentless children. Controversy immediately broke out over the governance of such a home. It soon became apparent that certain churchmen were more interested in strict organizational arrangements than in the needs of the homeless. Jesus took the opposite approach. He saw the human hurts and need first. A minister with this vision set out to secure funds. Despite considerable criticism, funds were raised and the home constructed. It continues even now to minister to the hurts and needs of the homeless.

A man of God had a vision for reaching into the community of unbelief. His approach, however, was not conventional. He knew the failure of traditional methods for reaching such people. Soon he heard objections from numerous quarters. He, like Jesus, had no desire to depart from the traditional simply to be different. But, also like Jesus, he was determined not to permit custom to stand in the way of a genuine human need, in this case bringing the light of God into communities of human darkness. He was subject to all sorts of pressures. But he did not leave. He presumed that what is important is bringing the love of God to men, not hairsplitting discussions over modes and methods. He was quite willing to go along with traditions whenever they did not stand in the way of sharing the love of God. That was uppermost with Jesus. And

84

so it must be with his disciples.

The rules, the laws of God, are crucial. But we don't interpret them aright, as some think, by continually struggling with the letter of the law. Jesus has shown us that if we are to come out at the right place it is necessary to discern the intent of the law. The one concerned with the letter of the law is correct—the Christian must be discerning—but he is wrong as to the manner. The discernment must scrutinize the intent, not the intricacies of casuistic deductions. The motive behind God's laws is his concern, his love, for man made in his image. God has given his law to help man, to show him how to attain the most out of life in this world and the world to come. The law of God must finally be interpreted in the light of the love of God. And his love is deep and unsearchable.

...to Be
COURAGEOUS 7

A number of people are turned off by religion—
humanistic religion that is. Religion that has become sterile, solidified, and shaped by the will of
man instead of the will of God. Unlike the "pure
and undefiled religion" (James 1:27), humanistic
religion has become defiled, authoritative, and demanding. They specify how much money is to be
used on special building programs and make considerable demands on one's time. Other people
react against religion which is very rigid and mechanical. There may be an insistence that one does
not drink coffee, cokes, or tea. Activities can't be
planned on Sundays, and holiday celebrations such
as Christmas are forbidden. Or perhaps the religion
consists mostly of stale traditions. There are traditional programs on anniversary days. There are
programs in honor of church officials. There are
the celebrations of national anniversaries. Other
religions are excited about flashy charismatic gifts

and discriminate among persons as to whether or not they have such gifts. Then there are religions which are mostly public relations. The people are obviously in it for the money and the organizations they have at their command. They relish flying around in Lear jets, building glittering churches and college buildings, and occupying plush offices.

Now when religion is criticized most religious people get very defensive. In fact, they may become aggressive and attempt to force their religion on persons such as children or employees who are subject to their power. We possibly get the feeling that all religious people are that way. Since we have consigned Jesus to a religious category we may have thought of him in that way, too.

It may therefore come as a surprise to find out that Jesus was not in favor of religion either, as we have described. Much of what people find wrong with religion Jesus also rejected. He did not come to establish religion nor to defend it. Jesus came to initiate the kingdom of God in the hearts and lives of men and women. The style of Jesus was not to be religious as the people of the country where he lived viewed religion. The center of it all for Jesus was

"You shall love the Lord your God with all your heart, and with all your soul, and with all your mind, and with all your strength. The second is this, You shall love your neighbor as yourself."

Mark 12:29-31

What most people call religion is false from the perspective of Jesus.

The Best Seats

Religion, as we have experienced it, is concerned with privilege, position, authority, and power. Religious leaders jockey for position. They carefully protect an established hierarchy. They spend considerable time devising ways to make the wheels of religion spin. Programs and buildings are planned; then means are devised to put pressure on the members so they participate. Sometimes people are given assessments indicating precisely how much they are to contribute. They are told to pay up or else. The threat held over their heads is expulsion from the religious body and eternal damnation by God. Or programs are designed for which numerous volunteers are needed. Considerable effort goes into arm twisting, exhorting, announcing, persuading, and occasionally downright threatening.

Jesus believed in dedication, commitment, and devotion to God. And, of course, religion talks as if that is what it's about. But many times it gets so bogged down in position and prestige that single-hearted devotion to God is somehow lost in the shuffle. Jesus laid the groundwork for forming groups for the banding of persons together for mutual encouragement and action. But central to this being together was service, love, and devotion—not prestige. So Jesus criticized religion in his time:

And in his teaching he said, "Beware of the scribes, who like to go about in long robes, and to have salutations in the market places and the best seats in the synagogues and the places of honor at feasts, who devour widows' houses and for a pretense make long prayers. They will receive the greater condemnation."

Mark 12:38-40

These "religious persons" had all the attributes we dislike about religion. They relished position and power. They made money demands because of their authoritative role. How did they "devour widows' houses"? A Jew would befriend a religious leader by inviting him to live with him and thereby supply his needs. But when the man would die, rather than leaving, the religious leader would remain with the widow and make excessive demands on her estate.

Sometimes we view religion as objectionable because it is just like everything else we are involved in. People are in it because it gives them a positoin of power from which to tell others what to do. It supplies the vehicle for reaping the benefits from the labors and sacrifices of others. Even the disciples of Jesus at one time thought involvement with him would bring privilege and authority. So they made a request, "Grant us to sit, one at your right hand and one at your left, in your glory" (10:37). The religion they had been involved with thought in those terms. But Jesus made it clear his priorities were elsewhere.

You know that those who are supposed to rule over the Gentiles lord it over them, and their great men exercise authority over them. But it shall not be so among you; but whoever would be great among you must be slave of all. For the Son of man also came not to be served but to serve, and to give his life as a ransom for many.

Mark 10:42-45

Jesus envisioned an amazing group of people who thought in terms of how they could love, help, share their lives, and serve each other. He had in mind a people who opened up their hearts to each other and to God. Jesus singled out the poor widow who "out of her poverty has put in everything she had, her whole living." (12:44) The body of believers Jesus envisioned is not out to tell people what to do, to watch and guard their every move, to work at keeping the hierarchy in line. It rather encourages single-hearted devotion to God. It makes opportunities for loving, sharing, and serving.

Opposing Mechanical Rules

It is not difficult to think of religion as a lot of insignificant discussion on a series of specific "do's and don'ts." In fact the word religion itself in Latin means a binding back, or holding back, or the enforcing of a series of restraints. We know religions which prescribe what to wear, what to eat and drink, what types of recreation and amusements are acceptible, if any, how to spend time and money, and a whole series of rituals and observances. Then in order to put teeth into these "do's and don'ts" Jesus is declared guardian and enforcer. But if one reads the life of Jesus carefully he discovers that's not where Jesus was.

In a sense we don't know much about Jesus and "religious rules." He did not react violently against them. He was not out to defy every rule. Likewise he gave little attention to creating rules.

Strangely enough, Jesus gave those close to him no instructions as to what sort of clothes to wear, what to eat and drink, or how to spend their spare time. If religion has to do with binding down, with rule making, then Jesus was not about religion.

"If religion has to do with binding down with rule making then Jesus was not about religion."

We find a few cases in which Jesus opposed the religious rule makers and enforcers. The Jews thought it an admirable trait of "religious people" to fast. In fact, they even had a series of rules about fasting, many of which had accumulated through the years. Now the Pharisees had no particular love for John the Baptist because he called them to repentance in preparation for the coming kingdom of God. But at least John and his disciples fasted. Jesus appeared religious, but he was not concerned to observe the outward signs of religion such as fasting. He was not against it, for he said the time would come when his disciples would fast (2:20). But he opposed fasting as a mechanical rule. The time for celebration, the time when the Son of God is present, is not the time of fasting. The time of fasting is when the Son has departed.

Eating With 'Defiled Hands'

Then there was the time the Pharisees watched the eating habits of Jesus' disciples. The Pharisees lived by very precise rules. They had regulations to apply to almost everything. They believed in a strict if not mechanical keeping of those regulations. They noticed that the disciples of Jesus ate without following the prescribed ritual of handwashing. They thought they had Jesus there. They sized him up as wishing to appear religious, and then they caught his disciples violating the rules of religion. But Jesus told the Pharisees they were not talking about a commandment of God, but a tradition (7:8). Jesus was careful to keep explicit laws of God. At least he was never accused of violating a law, with chapter and verse appended. But Jesus made it clear that a relationship with God had nothing to do with mechanically keeping food laws. "There is nothing outside a man which by going into him can defile him; but the things which come out of man are what defile him" (7:15). What counts is not details about rules, or keeping them mechanically. What counts is where a person's heart is. "For from within, out of the heart of man, come evil thoughts, fornication, theft, murder, adultery" (7:21).

"For Jesus what is demanded is a single-minded devotion to God and to loving one's neighbor as himself."

Jesus was not upset about rules. He was upset about people who thought that life and relationship with God has to do with the mechanics of rules and rule keeping. One reason we can say Jesus opposed religion is because rule keeping to many is precisely their main interest of religion. Jesus did not oppose rules and did not formulate rules of a mechanical sort. To do either would have been an elevation of rules to an importance Jesus did not see. For Jesus what is demanded is a single-minded devotion to God and to loving one's neighbor as himself. When that occurs, then rules fall in place. In fact, the laws of God are designed precisely for this purpose. The person who sees that loving God and following him singlemindedly what is required is, as Jesus put it, "not far from the kingdom of God" (12:34).

For They Feared Him

Jesus was not exactly one to be sentimental about the status quo. Traditions had no particular meaning for him one way or the other. For that reason he came into conflict with the religious leaders, because another attribute of religion is its inordinate, sometimes neurotic, compulsion to resist change. Maintaining the status quo involves a number of dimensions because religion is woven into the fabric of national, community, and family life. In the 1970s, when attitudes toward patriotism, divorce, law and order, women's rights, alcohol and drugs, and dress styles changed, religion felt the pinch more than anything else. This is because religion is one of the main societal forces for maintaining the status quo and praising and rewarding those so engaged.

It is only natural that those favoring change are alienated by religion. And again, because they view Jesus as "religious," they are also alienated by him because they place him among those who spend their days preserving the present order. But we might be surprised, in taking a closer look at Jesus, to discover that he reacted against the religion of his time precisely because it was dedicated to keeping things the way they were. It was clear that, if followed, he would upset the apple cart of religion. The religious leaders became deeply concerned. They "sought a way to destroy him; for they feared him, because all the multitude was astonished at his teaching" (11:18).

He Was Different

Consider the ways in which Jesus broke with religion. First of all, he affirmed that the status quo was to vanish and a new order appear. "The kingdom of God is at hand" (1:15). He demonstrated the kingdom's beginnings by casting out demons in the synagogue (1:25-28). He continued these works and his teaching and healing activities in houses, on the streets and roads, in the fields, on the hills, and on the sea. He healed people on the sabbath day (3:3). He forgave sin without religious rituals (2:7). He ate with persons not worthy according to the religious customs (2:16). He and his disicples did not fast (2:18). His disciples pulled grain on the sabbath (2:23). He ignored the feelings of his friends (3:21) and the criticisms of religious leaders (3:23). He ignored the requests of his mother and his brothers (3:32) and the ridicule of his townspeople (6:2). And notice—they all found fault with him because he was different.

If Jesus had been doing what everyone else was doing, if he had tried to maintain things just as they were, no one would have become excited. But what he did rocked the boat. He openly ignored certain religious traditions such as handwashing (7:2). He told one man that keeping the Ten Commandments was not enough (10:21). He charged that becoming rich is not the goal of life. The rich have the greater difficulty in entering the kingdom of God (10:23). He undercut the demands of family. "There is no one who has left house or brothers or sisters or mother or father or children or lands, for my sake and for the gospel, who will not receive a hundredfold now in this time" (10:29). He spoke out against the contemporary use of the temple (11:17). He told the religious leaders by way of parable that they rejected the true way of God as well as the One sent by God (12:1-11).

Standing For God

It is clear, therefore, that Jesus did not stand with religion. Religion is too tied up with nationalism and patriotism. Religion is too involved with laws and customs. It usually ends up being for what the community is for and against what it is against. Religion is too tied in with leadership, power struggles, and maintaining precise rituals and patterns of speech. It is too concerned to keep things the way they are. And religion is too tied up with motherhood, families, and demands.

Jesus opposed religion because it exercises most of its energy tying down the status quo to prevent it from escaping. Jesus was little concerned about the status quo one way or the other. He was concerned, however, with the way of God. God comes first, then one's neighbors. Countries, local communities, religious bodies, friends, and families—all of these have their place, but not as if they exist in their own right. Religion behaves toward itself and its environment as if it is sacrosanct in its own right. That is why religion seeks to maintain what is. But for Jesus nothing exists in its own right. For that reason neither change nor status quo is worshiped. Only God is worshiped. Religion comes out for the status quo. Radicals come out for change. Jesus comes out for neither. He comes out for God.

Discerning Religious 'Gifts'

Some people reject religion because of all the bizarre activities claimed in its name. Jesus did not embrace a wierd religion. It was obvious to him that people do all sorts of things in the name of religion that are actually inimical to God. If religion turns you off because of the many diverse opinions, move over and make room for Jesus! He sits with you.

We live in a time in which there has been an enormous outbreak of unusual "gifts" claimed in the name of Jesus. His ministry is claimed as a "charismatic," that is, a gift ministry. It is further argued that the way to identify the work of Jesus in the world is through locating "gifts." Furthermore, those with the flashiest gifts are the persons most of all to be admired. The person with no "gifts" is to be pitied, if not shamed. And one dare not question any gift, however strange or bizarre, since it is claimed in the name of God.

But Jesus stood at a different place. People in his time exercised many of the very gifts he enjoyed—for example, the casting out of demons (Matt. 12:27). Jesus did not launch a crusade to rid the world of all these unusual activities. But neither did he embrace them. He called for careful weighing and even rejecting. Many people would make false claims, though sometimes sincere, in the name of God and his Son:

And then if any one says to you, 'Look, here

is the Christ!' or 'Look, there he is!' do not believe it. False Christs and false prophets will arise and show signs and wonders, to lead astray, if possible, the elect. But take heed.

Mark 13:21-31

Jesus did indeed do mighty signs and wonders. He alienated many in his own time who considered him a fanatic. He also stated, according to a long ending of the Gospel of Mark, that some of the things he did would also characterize his disciples (16:17). But Jesus did not put these at the center of his ministry. Some kinds of religion thrive on the flashy, the unusual, the emotionally exciting. Jesus may have had a healing ministry, but the emphasis was not on gifts. The emphasis was the kingdom of God—that is, the serving, caring, giving love of God. The blind man to whom Jesus restored sight would have been more than pleased to give his testimony in the villages and the city. But in Jesus' thinking the kingdom of God does not depend on "gifts" testimonies. "And he sent him away to his home, saying, 'Do not even enter the village' " (8:26). Religion may thrive and grow on the excitement of "gifts." But the way of Jesus is not the way of religion. For Jesus, the kingdom of God can only grow where the excitement is created by the undying love of God.

Slave of All

It is clear that Jesus came seeking service, not privilege. He put together no power structures. He built no buildings. He founded no college. He launched no money-raising campaign. He purchased no vehicle of transportation. He had no plush office. He developed no channels for funneling money and influence. Some people, and rightly so, are upset at religion and religious figures because they are involved in all these activities. But this is not Jesus. This is religion.

Jesus, too, was repelled by religion as big business, as is clear from his action in the temple. He cared nothing for all the glitter and glamor of public acclaim and reward. His goal was single-minded. He came to establish the way of God on earth—the way of service—indeed, the way of the cross!

"Jesus opposed religion because religion thrives on self-serving ends."

Jesus turned upside down the way of religion in its grasp for privilege, for wealth, and power. The way of religion is the way of human organizations. These seek to lord it over persons. "Their great men exercise authority over them" (10:42). Jesus proposed the opposite:

> But it shall not be so among you; but whoever would be great among you must be your servant, and whoever would be first among you must be slave of all. For the Son of man also came not to be served but to serve, and to give his life as a ransom for many.
>
> Mark 10:43-45

Jesus opposed religion because religion thrives on self-serving ends. But the way of God is not self-serving. It is precisely the serving of others. It is so giving and serving that no answer can be given to religious functionaries.

And as soon as it was morning the chief priests, with the elders and scribes, and the whole council held a consultation; and they bound Jesus and led him away and delivered him to Pilate. And Pilate asked him, "Are you the king of the Jews?" And he answered him, "You have said so." And the chief priests accused him of many things. And Pilate again asked him, "Have you no answer to make? See how many charges they bring against you." But Jesus made no further answer, so that Pilate wondered.

Mark 15:1-5

No response can be made to religion. It cannot hear. Religion is on a different wave lengh. Where it rules, the life of Jesus is crowded out. Neither will religion understand Jesus' disciples. "But take heed to yourselves; for they will deliver you up to councils; and you will be beaten in the synagogues; and you will stand before governors and kings for my sake" (13:9). Jesus opposed religion because it is from man, not from God. The disciples of Jesus embrace God. They avoid religion.

...to Be
AUTHENTIC 8

In these days we are particularly sensitive to persons who give lip service to one set of values but who obviously live elsewhere. Such persons are phonies. They cover up their real self with a mouthful of platitudes. They are not personally involved in what they say. Or at times emotion comes through, but it's difficult to locate the origin. What these people are does not match what they say. They mouth the ideas one expects from someone in their position but there is no ring of truth from the deep, inner recesses of their being. They are not real people. Their dress is phony. Their work ethic is phony. They defend the status quo even though they know its weaknesses. They put up a phony front to impress people, and they support other phonies to keep the shell from caving in. They simply don't come off as real persons. We usually wouldn't care to strike up friendships among this sort. We want to be around people who are authentic.

Jesus also preferred authentic persons. He turned away from the phonies and praised the real people. Now we may or may not agree with what he thought real, but obviously he believed that people should live what they really are. He wasn't impressed with the status seekers who draw from life every ounce of privilege and publicity. He withstood those types. He did nothing to court their favor or to attain position among them, even though they enjoyed and could dole out numerous privileges.

Some of these persons saw themselves as standing in high favor with God. They believed they alone understood and observed his ways. Jesus found them insincere. He knew they were in it for the praise of man rather than the approval of God. Jesus side-stepped such people whenever he could. He found his place mainly among those without fame and who made no claims. The people he praised were those who gave themselves to God with no concern for the praise of men. They were often unheralded persons. The religious leaders in vying for position were too busy to notice them. What they did made no great public stir, but God loved them because they gave themselves in single-hearted devotion.

A man and his wife in their seventies had a friend who was a nurse in a major hospital. She informed them of persons with special needs. Perhaps they were from out of town and were without a place to stay. Perhaps they needed someone to sit with them in the hospital, or to take care of a child or an invalid parent. Whatever the need, this dedicated couple assisted. Even people close to them did not know all the things they did because they were very reluctant to tell even when asked. They desired no praise or credit. They did it because they were committed to Christ. He had helped them and showed that life consists in helping. They were faithful and active members of the body. But they had no special position nor desired one. They made no pretense about their faith. They obviously lived what they really were. They were authentic.

'And For A Pretense'

In his teaching at the temple, Jesus spoke bluntly about those who made a pretense of piety. Mark reports two consecutive episodes in which Jesus first criticized phonies, then praised a real person.

Jesus attacked the scribes because of the blatant sham of their actions:

> And in his teaching he said, "Beware of the scribes, who like to go about in long robes, and to have salutations in the market places and the best seats in the synagogues and the places of honor at feasts, who devour widows' houses and for a pretense make long prayers. They will receive the greater condemnation."

> Mark 12:38-40

According to Jesus, at least some of the scribes were "religious" not to serve God, but to obtain prestige and favoritism. They flourished; they lived well; the accolades of men and women came their way; but in the end time, according to Jesus, they would be condemned by God. They wore long white robes, the dress of persons with power and authority. The average person on the street wore brown or other colors. It was a custom that whenever a scribe walked through the market-place, people were expected to arise and address them as "Rabbi," "Father," or "Master." According to Jesus the scribes relished these greetings. They eagerly anticipated their daily forays into the market.

When a scribe attended a synagogue service he was given a seat of honor at the front. He sat with his face toward the congregation and his back to the chest where the Torah was kept. Scribes did not hesitate in accepting this honor and did nothing to discourage it. When important Jews gave feasts they considered it a special show of graciousness to invite a distinguished scribe and his pupils. They assigned them the choice seats, even passing over parents and other aged persons. Apparently scribes relished such invitations. They flattered the host, anticipating future dinner invitations.

The scribes had little concerned for the needy. They spent their time basking in the sunlight of the praise of men. Some went so far as to abuse the courtesies extended. It was the rule among the Jews that a scribe could not have an income. But he was permitted to accept gifts, and invitations to live with those of means. Jesus charged that scribes overextended such hospitality. They even continued to live with widows after the death of their husbands. It was this practice which Jesus had in mind when he accused them of devouring "widows' houses." The scribes prayed lengthy prayers, taking pains to be seen and heard so as to enhance their image as pious ones. The overriding motive in their life was the approval of men, not of God. They had even less interest in helping their fellows. In fact, they sometimes encouraged rules which barred helping the needy, such as the principle of "corban" (7:11-13).

They lived to enhance their own privileges and interests. The hollowness of it all was that God required exactly the opposite from ancient days. Seven hundred years earlier Micah told God's people, "He has showed you, O Man, what is good; and what does the Lord require of you but to do justice, and to love kindness, and to walk humbly with your God?" (Micah 6:8). Despite this charge, and the fact that they ignored it, these scribes professed to be God's sons. They were phonies.

This Poor Widow

There were, however, authentic people on the scene. Once Jesus sat with the disciples in the temple in a place where they could see the Jews placing money in the treasury vessels. That was in itself a study in humanity. A poor widow came along. Jesus singled her out. He offered her as the paradigm of an authentic godly person.

> And he sat down opposite the treasury, and watched the multitude putting money into the treasury. Many rich people put in large sums. And a poor widow came, and put in two copper coins, which made a penny. And he called his disciples to him, and said to them, 'Truly, I say to you, this poor widow has put in more than all those who are contributing to the treasury. For they all contributed out of their abundance; but she out of her poverty has put in everything she had, her whole living."
>
> Mark 12:41-44

The money placed in these containers was to be used for religious and public purposes. The public spirited Jew considered it his obligation to contribute. At the same time, he desired recognition for his giving and made it as obvious as possible. Tithing was, of course, required by the Old Testament law. There were thirteen trumpet-shaped containers for contributions, located against the wall of the Court of Women. As Jesus and the disciples watched they heard the clinking coins of the rich. But these wealthy persons dropped in only a pittance out of their superfluity.

"What counts is not the amount, nor the percentage given, but the unmixed dedication of life and one's resources to God."

Then a widow came along who was in dire poverty. She dropped in two copper coins which together were worth about one-half cent in American currency. Jesus noticed, but likely no one else did. Obviously the religious leaders and the influential wealthy paid scant attention. Her gift was nothing. Why should anyone give it a second thought? But it was a real gift because of the commitment and sacrifice represented by it. The woman, according to Jesus, put in "everything she had, her whole living." She did not give out of the desire for praise. No one would compliment her; her gift was not enough. The reason she contributed was pure and simple. It was out of love and devotion to God. She was an authentic person in the sight of God. In fact, what reward she might receive would have to come from him, since men ignored her

105

action. If they had noticed they would have thought her irresponsible if not foolish for squandering what little she had. She could have spent it on food. But Jesus didn't see it that way. He considered it a whole-hearted commitment to God. Not that God demanded it; but single-minded dedication is what pleases him most.

Aristotle probably thought of giving in the manner of most humans. He argued that only the person who has great wealth can qualify as a magnanimous giver. The person who has little and gives much is either a showoff or foolish.

This puts it out of the question for a poor man to be magnificent. He has not got the wherewithal to spend large sums in a way to do him credit, and if he tries it, he will make an exhibition of himself. He is spending beyond his means and in a way he ought not, since his behavior will be morally right only if he spends in the right way. Those for whom we regard it as right and proper to make such donations are people with suitable incomes derived from property acquired by their own exertions or inherited from their ancestors or relations; or they may be persons of good family or high distinction or otherwise specially qualified.

The Nicomachean Ethics, Book IV, 2

Jesus turned Aristotle's observations upside down. For him the person who is to be praised is the person who makes a deep commitment to God rather than the one who gives much. The committed person is praiseworthy even though he depletes what he has. What counts is singular devotion to

God. Such dedication may come from a rich person, someone of moderate means, or a poor person. What counts is not the amount, nor the percentage given, but the unmixed dedication of life and one's resources to God.

A Christian worked for a concrete tile company. It was hard work and he put in long hours. He was in his thirties, had four children, and was buying a house. He drove a seven-year-old-car. His family was active in the congregation, but since he was an unsophisticated manual laborer, and from another region, he was not particularly admired by others in the body. One of the brothers had financial reverses and needed help. Other individuals could have assisted, but didn't. The brother who seemed to have meager resources said he would lend him $500. He said it did not matter whether he paid him back since he had the money and didn't need it. He said he was glad to do it and was sure that God would see that he himself had what he needed.

She Has Done A Beautiful Thing

The same point about single-hearted devotion was made by Jesus in regard to the woman who anointed his head at Bethany. In his final week, Jesus stayed at the home of Simon the leper who lived in Bethany, about four miles southeast of Jerusalem's city wall. On one occasion, as they sat down to eat, "a woman came with an alabaster jar of ointment of pure nard, very costly, and she broke the jar and poured it over his head" (14:3-4). The jar, with its contents, could have been sold for as much as a full year's wages. It may have been a family heirloom. The container was made of alabaster, a soft, brittle material. The woman broke the neck of the flask and poured the fragrant contents over Jesus' head. Anointing guests' heads with oil before a meal was a normal procedure and considered a special courtesy to those invited. But in this particular case the meal had already begun and the ointment was unusually expensive. Certain of those present, including some of the disciples, were indignant. "Why was the ointment thus wasted! For this ointment might have been sold for more than three hundred denarii, and given to the poor" (14:5).

Their remark was phony. They didn't care that much for the poor. They thought it was a waste. But what the woman did was a supreme act of appreciation. She earnestly wanted to show that Jesus meant so much to her that he was worthy of her unlimited devotion. Jesus recognized the sincerity of her act. So he said to the critics, "Let her alone; why do you trouble her! She has done a beautiful thing to me" (14:6). There are always people around to help. One can always defend letting an opportunity pass to show honor on the ground there are so many to praise and so many to whom one is indebted. But when this woman saw a singular meritorious life which obviously exhibited God himself, she was moved to act. Jesus understood, and came to her defense.

> For you always have the poor with you, and whenever you will, you can do good to them; but you will not always have me. She has done what she could; she has anointed my body beforehand for burying.
>
> Mark 14:7-8

The woman at Bethany stands out as a real person because of the genuineness of her love and

108

feeling for Jesus. She didn't hide her appreciation, nor hold back on practical grounds. She apparently anticipated his impending death. In that light her action was especially fitting. She showed how much she cared by anointing his body beforehand. He was the Anointed One and she showed her commitment by her act. The sharp barbs of the others, their real concerns hidden, were brazenly crass, if not phony. Jesus admired those who genuinely gave of themselves, holding nothing back, since God gives himself in the same way.

'Whoever Gives You A Cup Of Water'

Jesus did not care for what was flashy and showy, but hollow. He praised what may have sometimes seemed inconsequential but was actually authentic. Notice, for example, how many of the people Jesus praised were women. Men usually received the accolades and awards, even when wives and secretaries do most of the work. Jesus gave credit to persons who ordinarily do not receive credit, those who do what they do out of love or dedication. Jesus believed that the future lay with the genuine, however small or apparently unimportant.

The parables about the kingdom indicate the concrete manner in which Jesus went with the real rather than the powerful. The kingdom is like a grain of mustard seed which is small and unimpressive. It is "the smallest of all the seeds on earth; yet when it is sown it grows up and becomes the greatest of all shrubs" (4:31-32). The kingdom of God proliferates, not because of what is impressive and magnificent, but from what is authentic.

In another parable Jesus spoke of certain per-

109

sons who immediately respond when they first hear the good news. For a time they are excited and grow. But after a few weeks they start to whither. They "have no root in themselves, but endure for a while; then, when tribulation or persecution arises on account of the word, immediately they fall away" (4:17). The kingdom of God does not grow from that which is facile, facade, or phony. It can only flourish and produce when the soil is fertile and deep. Those who make much noise but do nothing add little. The kingdom depends on persons who do the work of the kingdom quietly and are little noticed. So Christians sing:

How silently, how silently the wondrous gift is given?
So God imparts to human hearts the blessings of His heaven!
No ear may hear His coming; but in this world of sin,
Where meek souls will receive Him, still the dear Christ enters in.

Becoming Authentic

Jesus was not impressed with discussions of who is the greatest. He found them hollow. Greatness is ordinarily determined by position. The person who has the most influence wins out. Jesus saw such analyses of greatness as a sham, because thereby self-interest is served rather than helpfulness to others. On one occasion the disciples fell into a heated discussion. Jesus wanted to know what it was all about. They were embarrassed and said nothing. They already sensed that Jesus was not impressed by human measures of greatness. Jesus called the twelve and said to them "If any

110

one would be first, he must be last of all and servant to all." He then led a child to the middle of the disciples. Taking the child up in his arms he said, "Whoever receives one such child in my name receives me; and whoever receives me, receives not me but him who sent me" (9:37). God is not interested in pretensions to greatness and power. He is interested in the one who is willing to turn aside and help the least significant human being, even a child. One becomes real in the eyes of God by serving even the most inconsequential.

"Authentic persons by Jesus' standards were those with singlehearted devotion to God."

The real disciples of the Lord turn their back on striving for position. From the standpoint of Jesus those who count only high and mighty activities worthy of their time are inauthentic. The real persons serve, regardless of how insignificant or paltry the deed may seem. "For truly, I say to you, whoever gives you a cup of water to drink because you bear the name Christ, will by no means lose his reward" (9:41).

Authentic persons by Jesus' standards were those with singlehearted devotion to God. Jesus minced no words in reacting to the aspirations of James and John for positions of power.

> You know that those who are supposed to rule over the Gentiles lord it over them. But it shall not be so among you; but whoever would be great among you must be your ser-

vant, and whoever would be first among you must be slave of all.''

Mark 10:42-44

Jesus searches for those available to serve, to help the needy, however insignificant. That was his own life. He showed the way. He was noted for putting his life where his mouth was. He invites us to shed our phoniness and become authentic. We do this by surrendering all to him. If we try, he will supply the power!

COMPASSIONATE 9

Jesus himself summed up the intent of his ministry in these words: "For the Son of man also came not to be served but to serve, and to give his life as a ransom for many" (10:45). Why did Jesus come to serve? Were the mighty works which characterized his ministry his means of serving? Do the miracles mean, as the people of Nain said when Jesus raised a widow's son from death, "God has come to help his people"? (Luke 7:16, NIV).

And He Had Compassion On Them

Mark doesn't always tell us what prompted an action of Jesus, but sometimes he does. The most explicit explanation is that he helped people because *he cared*.

A leper, one of those exiled from normal human contacts, approached Jesus "Beseeching him, and kneeling said to him, 'If you will, you can make me clean.' " Jesus was touched by the desperate yet expectant plea of the man. So Mark reports, "Moved with pity, he stretched out his hand and touched him, and said to him, "I will; be clean" (1:41). The *New English Bible* reads "in warm indignation," an accurately phrased translation. Jesus was stirred at the debilitating encroachment of the leprosy. He healed the man because he was upset over the harshness of the affliction. He was moved out of pity, because of the outrage of it all.

When the word spread abroad of Jesus' healing powers, people flocked in from towns and villages. He healed person after person, but they kept coming. Finally the pressure mounted and there was no time even to eat. So Jesus said to his disciples, "Come away by yourselves to a lonely place, and rest awhile" (6:31). They went away in a boat. But those on the shore noticed in what direction they headed, and, running on foot along the shore, met the boat as it landed. Jesus needed to relax, but he was overwhelmed by the urgency of the people. "And he had compassion on them, because they were like sheep without a shepherd; and he began to teach them many things" (6:31). Jesus interrupted his journey, not to influence the crowd, not to impress them with his powers, but because his heart reached out.

Later, Jesus was in a wilderness area teaching and healing. Many were there. They had come without provisions, and several had been with him for three days. Jesus, aware of their plight, called the disciples and told them,

> I have compassion on the crowd, because they have been with me now three days, and have nothing to eat; and if I sent them away hungry to their homes, they will faint on the

way; and some of them have come a long way."

Mark 8:2-3

Jesus recognized that what a man believes counts, but that the demands of the body aren't inconsequential. The crowd was hungry. The love of Jesus—his compassion—determined his action. Jesus came not to astound or amaze but to help the hurting, the down and out, those looking to God for deliverance.

The Old Testament depicts God as having compassion for his people. When they cry to him out of misery he answers (Exod. 2:23-25; Judg. 3:9). He is a God who seeks to "bring good tidings to the afflicted; bind up the broken-hearted, proclaim liberty to the captives, and the opening of prison to those who are bound" (Isa. 61:1). Jesus has compassion because he is the Son of a God of compassion. He is our model for doing deeds of compassion.

People Came From Every Quarter

Not only was the compassion of Jesus intense; it reached in all directions. While Jesus helped only a limited number of those alive during his few short years, he did so without restrictive formula. His compassion went everywhere. The main criteria seemed to be the request for help. He assisted people of all sorts, in all kinds of places, for varying lengths of time, in all kinds of ways. His compassion was obvious throughout.

Jesus was involved with all kinds of people. He assisted persons of all social classes. He helped outcasts, such as lepers (1:4), blind beggars (10:46), and people with evil spirits (5:1-20). He

115

assisted persons of means, or as we would label them, middle class—for example the woman who had a flow of blood and had spent considerable money (5:25). He also helped people of the ruling or upper class, such as Jairus who was a ruler of the synagogue (5:22). We have examples of him responding to persons of many occupations—tax collectors (3:15), religious leaders (5:22), housewives (7:25), fishermen (1:16), prostitutes (14:3-9; 16:9), and farmers (5:14-20). He showed compassion upon all age levels, beginning with children (10:13), then young men and women (9:20; 5:23), and adults (5:25). The aged were never singled out, but they were no doubt among those who ate of the loaves and the fishes (6:35; 8:1). He responded to the pleas for help from both women (7:25) and men (5:22). He helped Jews (5:22), Gentiles (7:25), his disciples (4:37-41), and those with whom he had had no prior contact (1:40). These are the particular people we know about. If we knew the specifics of those present when "the whole city gathered" (1:33) we could no doubt complete the spectrum.

"The love of God knows no place nor time, and neither did the compassion of Jesus."

Jesus is usually depicted as being by the seaside or in the country with people streaming to him. But he had no formula as to where he helped or whether he went to people or they came to him. He, like God, had compassion on men and women whenever they cried out, regardless of the circumstances.

Jesus cast out demons in a synagogue (1:23), in

front of Peter's house (1:33), and in a cemetery (5:2). He healed persons in a house (1:31), on a road (1:40), in a synagogue (3:1), in villages, cities, the country, market places (6:56), and outside a village (8:23). Sometimes he went to people (1:38-39), but sometimes people came to him (5:22) and took him to the one to be healed (5:24). Sometimes people who couldn't make it by themselves were carried to him (2:3). Many times he just happened to run into someone in need (11:46). The love of God knows no place nor time, and neither did the compassion of Jesus.

Compassion Without Formula

The compassion of the disciple of Jesus also is without formula. A servant of the Lord received a call in the middle of the day from a young man who planned to take his own life. The servant had a busy schedule, but he stopped everything and talked to the young man at length on the telephone. Finally he persuaded him to let him come over to his apartment. While there the talks continued and the would-be suicide was taken to the hospital. The servant spent as much time as possible with him and invited a few trusted others to come down as time permitted. After two days the young man felt better but still exhibited severe problems and still talked as if he might take his life. The servant had to make a trip to several cities. He decided it was important that the young man go along. It was not easy. The young man was very demanding. But the servant took him because he was aware that the compassion of Jesus knew no time or place.

Jesus likewise had no rule of thumb whereby he

determined how long to help those with a problem. Sometimes Jesus' help was immediate, and as far as we know that was the last time Jesus saw the person—as in the case of the woman with a flow of blood (5:25). With others, Jesus had occasional contacts. In Bethany Jesus ate at the house of Simon the leper (14:3). This Simon was no doubt cured by Jesus on a previous occasion. Since he lived in Bethany he may have been the husband of Martha, or possibly the father of Martha, Mary, and Lazaras.

But with a number of people Jesus maintained a continuing relationship from the beginning of his ministry. Among these were the twelve, and also various women including Mary Magdalene, Mary the mother of James, and Salome (16:1). Above all, we recognize that Jesus' heart reached out to people whenever and wherever they had needs. With some he worked in depth, for they were involved in laying the foundation of the kingdom of God. With these he would be forever.

> So then the Lord Jesus, after he had spoken to them, was taken up into heaven, and sat down at the right hand of God. And they went forth and preached everywhere, while the Lord worked with them and confirmed the message by the signs that attended it.
>
> Mark 16:19-20

What Do These Words Mean?

The compassion of Jesus likewise becomes obvious when one scrutinizes the purpose of his mighty works. It is important to notice that with one exception all the miracles of Jesus were loving acts of helpfulness. The miracles prove that a loving God

118

has entered history in Jesus. The emphasis is as much on the compassion that shines through, as the divinity.

Professor Harold Schilling, former head of the Physics Department and later Dean of the Graduate School at the Pennsylvania State University, tells of a conference of physicists and theologians he attended in Germany in the 1950s. Those were the days when the views of Rudolf Bultmann overpowered the theological scene in Germany. Bultmann held that twentieth century man could only believe that the causes of everything in this world were from within this world. In other words, none of the events which had happened or were happening are caused by God. The subject of miracles kept coming up at the conference. In the non-programmed part of the conference the physicists tended to gravitate together, as did the theologians. Finally, toward the end of the conference, one of the physicists spoke up. "You theologians keep telling us physicists we can't believe in the miracles of the New Testament because we are modern, scientific men. But we can! That isn't our problem. Our problem is, we want to know what the miracles mean, and we were hoping you could tell us."

The question is a significant one. What do the miracles mean? If we put this question to Mark we come up with a clear answer. Jesus performed unusual feats out of compassion, but also in hope that his followers would come to believe in his Sonship.

These purposes emerge when we examine in some detail the nature of Jesus' feats. The mighty works of Jesus (6:2) can be categorized into five groups. (1) Jesus raised the dead, as in the case of the daughter of Jairus. (2) He cast out demons; for example, from the possessed lad with whom the disciples had failed (9:14-29). (3) He healed a number of people; for example, the man who culdn't hear or speak (7:32-37). (4) He fed hungry thousands (8:1-10). (5) He delivered the disciples from the storms on the sea (4:37-41).

"The miracles mean that in Jesus a God of love has visited his people."

In each of these five types of extraordinary deeds Jesus remedied a crucial need. They were not designed for exhibitionism. Jesus was not out to prove his divinity. He was not out for revenge. Neither did he perform simply to satisfy the whims of those whom he liked. In each case Jesus had a worthy end. People needed help and they received it. The miracles mean that in Jesus a God of love has visited his people. The kingdom of God, the place where God rules, has arrived.

Mark reports one event which does not fit the mold. As Jesus left Bethany and headed for Jerusalem he came upon a fig tree. He was hungry and looked for figs, but finding none, said to the tree, "May no one ever eat from you again" (11:14). The next morning Peter, remembering the curse, looked at the tree and found it withered (11:21). This obviously was not an act of love. No one was helped by the withering of the tree. Just why Jesus cursed the tree is not immediately obvious. The likely reason is that Jesus did it to show his disciples that faith can accomplish the impossible (11:21-25). He did it, not out of vindictiveness, nor to raise eyebrows, but to demonstrate the power of faith. By probing in greater depth it is also obvious that something is being proclaimed here about the role of the temple and the Jewish people in the continual purposes of God. By this action Jesus announced that God has rejected Israel because she has misapplied his gifts and has ceased to bear fruit. Furthermore, the work of God for the salvation of his people has shifted from the temple to Jesus. Prayers and faith, therefore, are the route to God, not temple sacrifices and ceremonies. Regardless, Jesus did not destroy the fig tree simply to astound or to demonstrate his divine powers.

Being Compassionate

One of the basic traits of Jesus is his compassion for men. He came to serve. He was not interested in self-achievement. He was interested in spreading abroad the love of God. The nature of his works show he was concerned about the outcast, the distraught, the needy, and the hungry. These are the concerns of God himself. Jesus hoped that in what he did, his disciples would see the work of God. If so, they would get the message of God's concerns. The way of God is the way of love and service.

We, too, are asked to see these concerns of Jesus, our model, as matters that are central to the universe. God, through the Son, calls us to be persons of compassion. He calls us to be such persons because by doing so we become attuned to the universe. Love and compassion are central to the universe because those are the traits of the creator God. The universe is what it is, because of God. In our quiet way, sometimes in remote places away from the attention of others we go where the needy cry out. We leave the paneled walls and padded pews for the other side of the tracks where people despair in their wretchedness. We leave our well-ordered worship for the places where life is seamy and dirty. These days we may find such places among the rich as well as the poor, the educated as well as the ignorant. Like Jesus we do what we do, not for prestige or power, but in order to help men and women, all of whom are made in the image of God. We are able to help, not because we have great self-generated powers, but because we needed such help when he found us. "We love because he first loved us."

A young couple graduated from college. Rather than securing a job immediately, they elected to stay at the school so he could do graduate work. While in school they had a baby daughter. Since they didn't have much money he secured a position as a teacher. After two years they decided that Jesus called them to other involvement. So they pulled up stakes, without the promise of a position and moved to be with a group in the northeast who are ministering in the downtown area of an old city to those who have lost their direction on the path of life. The job they had hoped for was not forthcoming. But the couple continues to minister to the estranged, the unruly, the wayward, the poor. They have taken up a ministry of compassion. In this manner they are holding up a light in the kingdom of darkness. Jesus' ministry of compassion continues even through us.

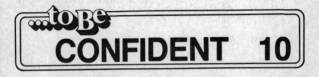

...to Be CONFIDENT 10

We know people who come on strong. At first glance they strike us as persons of authority. But as we get to know them we find them insecure. They apparently come on strong as compensation for their own inferior self-image. Others we run into seem straight-forward and courageous. They have a swagger in their talk and actions. But as we get to know them we discover they are attention seekers. They do many flamboyant and risky things so people will notice and talk. For them, the most cruel of fates would be to go unnoticed—to be a nobody.

Still others we meet cultivate a first impression of boldness if not brusqueness. They do so because underneath they are really soft-hearted and susceptible to almost any sales pitch or sob story. Some are impressive because they are involved in twenty-three different projects and organizations and seem to get an enormous amount of work done. But the more we get to know them we learn that their fast pace covers a fear of inadequacy. They have a rather low opinion of their abilities so they go around in frenzied activity, hoping that at least if they do several things they will be noticed somewhere. Some such people are afraid to stop because they don't really know who they are. If they paused they would have to face that question, and that would be too painful. People may therefore on the surface exude boldness, authority, and over-achieving, but still be afflicted with a low threshold of self-confidence.

A Person Of Confidence

Jesus was remembered for his authority, his power, his boldness, his achievements. But a further characteristic stood out. He was a person of confidence and certainty. He never went about frenzied and unsettled because there was so much to do. There was never any uncontrolled, high-strung, irritable outburst. He came on as a man who knew who he was and what he was doing. There was a calm certitude about his life. He never complained about how he had no feeling for his work, that it seemed so remote, so meaningless. We have no reports that he asked people what they thought of a particular statement or action to obtain their approbation and hence their reassurance. As far as we know Jesus did not spend long hours in self evaluation worrying as to whether his life was going in the right direction or whether in a specific case he had done the right thing. He was never so uncertain about his life that he sought revenge on those who rejected him. He was always calm and confident.

'Follow me!'

Jesus was confident when he made a request. The call of the disciples shows that Jesus without hesitation got straight to the point.

> And passing along by the Sea of Galilee, he saw Simon and Andrew the brother of Simon casting a net in the sea; for they were fishermen. And Jesus said to them "Follow me and I will make you become fishers of men." And immediately they left their nets and followed him.

Mark 1:16-18

No doubt there is more to this story than Mark tells us. Luke and John both speak of prior contacts. But all alike report that when Jesus selected his disciples he did not weasel nor wheedle. He made his request with an air of assurance. He did not approach the matter with tried and calculated manipulative devices. He had not studied tactics by which to ascertain whether his client was on the verge of purchase. He did not fidget. He did not fumble, unsure of just how or when to say what was on his mind. His mouth was not dry, nor his voice high pitched. He spoke with confidence, believing that his request would be granted.

It was the same when Jesus sent the disciples for a colt on which to ride into Jerusalem toward the climax of his ministry (11:2-3). He was unperturbed lest someone object, "If any one says to you, 'Why are you doing this?' say, 'The Lord has need of it and will send it back here immediately.' "

In the same confidence Jesus instructed the disciples in respect to passover arrangements:

And he sent two of his disciples, and said to them, "Go into the city, and a man carrying a jar of water will meet you; follow him, and wherever he enters, say to the household, 'The Teacher says, Where is my guest room, where I am to eat the passover with my disciples.' And he will show you a large upper room furnished and ready; there prepare for us."

Mark 14:12-14

" ...He apparently saw prayer as supplying long-range power, rather than a crutch in the moment of crisis."

Jesus did not beat around the bush. He came straight to the point. When he asked, he received. He was, of course, on more than one occasion rejected. But in these cases he had not asked. He sometimes let people respond as they would, for example, the young rich man who called Jesus "Good Teacher" (10:17-22). Jesus invited him to "Come, follow me" (10:21). But Jesus was not expectant then and he made no effort to impede the man when he decided to leave.

Jesus proceeded with dispatch once he made up his mind to do something. When confronted with a task he did not doodle or puzzle. He had no formulas or rituals. He did not even always pray before plunging into an especially sticky situation. He believed in prayer and prayed frequently. He taught his disciples to pray. But he apparently saw prayer as supplying long-range power, rather than a crutch in the moment of crisis.

Jesus went with his disciples to Peter's home. Peter's mother-in-law lay sick with fever. They told Jesus and he did not hesitate. He did not pause to work out a formula for beginning. He went straight to the ill woman. "He . . . took her hand and lifted her up, and the fever left her; and she served them" (1:31).

Then there was the Syro-phoenician woman who begged Jesus to heal her daughter. At first Jesus refused: "Let the children first be fed" (7:27). But she persisted. Jesus had not seen the daughter. He knew nothing about her. He simply said to the mother, "The demon has left your daughter! And she went home, and found the child lying in the bed, and the demon gone" (7:29-30). Jesus did no preliminaries. He had no later doubts. He was confident that when he spoke, it was done. And it was!

Facing Rejection With Confidence

One of the most impressive things about Jesus was the manner in which he responded to rejection. He didn't feel threatened. He didn't feel inadequate or inferior. He didn't sneak off to a hole and pull it in after him. He didn't quit, saying, "Well if that's the way you feel, you can have it." He didn't threaten or lash out at the offenders. He called down no lightning. He did not grit his teeth and say under his breath, "They'll have to put up with me whether they like it or not."

Soon after Jesus began his ministry he was confronted by a series of actions challenging his purpose and being. First, some friends looked on, saw all the people, shook their head and declared, "He is beside himself" (3:21). They considered him demon possessed. (See John 10:20, in which madness is equated with demon possession—"He has a demon, and he is mad.") Jesus simply ignored the remark and continued his work. As far as we know he did not approach the task with any less energy, thinking to himself, "Well, perhaps I should think this through again."

"His concern was not in examining, but in doing the will of God."

The truth is that Mark tells us very little about how Jesus felt. He does tell us of Jesus' pity, compassion, and anger, and fatigue. In the garden of Gethsemane shortly before his death Jesus spoke of his soul being "very sorrowful" (14:34). We aren't told, however, how he felt about these friends. We only know what he did upon hearing their sharp remarks. He kept on doing what he had done previously. From what we know of the Gospels, Jesus was not deeply introspective in the modern sense. In the Gospel of Mark Jesus says very little about motives or feelings. In the Sermon on the Mount in Matthew, Jesus condemns hate and lust as just as sinful as the acts produced by them. But for the most part Jesus was not that concerned with the feelings or the emotions. He did not psychologize about "mountain peak" and "valley" experiences. His concern was not in examining but in doing the will of God.

But back to Mark 3, when Jesus' friends accused him of being "beside himself." Some of the scribes added insult to injury, saying, "He is possessed by Beelzebul and by the prince of demons he casts out demons" (3:22). That was two blows in a row. But

Jesus didn't fold. He did not lash back. He remained calm and collected, and responded with a question. He had confidence in the power of reason and his own use of it:

> And he called them to him, and said to them in parables, "How can Satan cast out Satan? If a kingdom is divided against itself, that kingdom cannot stand. And if a house is divided against itself, that house will not be able to stand. And if Satan has risen up against himself and is divided he cannot stand, but is coming to an end. But no one can enter a strong man's house and plunder his goods, unless he first binds the strong man; then indeed he may plunder his house.
>
> Mark 3:23-27

Through reason Jesus made it clear that if his power derived from demonic sources, his accomplishments were destructive to those forces—which simply did not make sense. Later in Jerusalem, Jesus carried on lengthy disputes with the scribes, the Pharisees, and the Sadducees. They spoke about paying the Roman tax, the question of resurrection, and which is the greatest of the commandments (12:13-34). Jesus had confidence not only in what he did, but also in what he said, and in his reasoning powers.

Family Opposition

And if two blows weren't enough, Jesus' own family added a third. His mother and brothers came and sent for him. Apparently they, too, thought him possessed. "And his mother and his brothers came; and standing outside they sent to him and called him." The implication of their request is "Quit making a spectacle of yourself. You are causing us great embarrassment. Come on home."

It would take a person who really knew who he was to stand up in the face of these criticims. But despite these unfavorable charges Jesus didn't appear threatened. There was no crack in his armor of self-identity. He had been affirmed by the Father. He knew who he was and why he was doing what he was doing. He had inner certitude which made him impervious to criticism and rejection. Ridicule from one's family hurts deeply. But Jesus had no harsh words for them. He simply told the crowd, "Here are my mother and my brothers! Whoever does the will of God is my brother, and sister, and mother." (3:34-35) Such confidence is difficult to come upon.

A college girl wanted to spend the summer with an outreach group. The group spent the summer in New England telling the good news of the love of God in Jesus, and loving and serving his children. She wanted to do this because she heard the call of Jesus, "Go into all the world and preach the gospel to the whole creation" (16:15). Her parents were opposed to her desires. They were active church members but they didn't wish their daughter to be that committed. They tried as best they could to dissuade her. They told her they would not help her, and furthermore that they would not supply any of her needs for school the next fall if she went. It was not an easy decision. But she decided the prior claim fell with the Son. Because he had spoken, she went forth with confidence. Brothers and sisters in the Lord supplied her needs as well as helped her return to school in the fall.

130

They Begged Him To Depart

Perhaps as difficult a request as any is a demand that one leave. There was the time Jesus exorcised the demons from the man who lived in the cave-tombs in the country of the Gerasenes. At the demons' request Jesus permitted them to enter a herd of swine feeding on the hillside. But when they had entered the swine, the herd rushed down the steep bank into the sea and drowned (5:13). The swine herders were astounded and fled that awesome place as fast as possible. As they came upon the people in the country and towns they related these strange happenings. A large group of the curious soon collected. They saw the demoniac and he was normal. "And they were afraid" (5:15). They didn't know what to make of it all, and the best they knew to do was ask Jesus to leave. "And they began to beg Jesus to depart from their neighborhood" (5:17).

Jesus did not argue. He was not upset. He took it all in stride. Mark simply reports, "And as he was getting into the boat, the man who had been possessed with demons begged him that he might be with him." Jesus took it as no affront that he was requested to leave. The request was their prerogative. He had other work. As far as we can tell, Jesus did not feel threatened by refusals. He did not hesitate to accept no for an answer.

After being away for some days Jesus returned to his own city. While gone he had done many mighty works which he had not attempted while at home. On the sabbath he went with his townspeople to the synagogue where he taught. Those who heard were astonished. They had to admit he had acquired unusual powers, but they were skeptical.

"Is this not the carpenter, the son of Mary and brother of James . . . and they took offense at him" (6:2-3). Most of us who return home after having been away for the first time hope to be favorably recognized. Most everyone relishes the headline, "Hometown boy makes good." But Jesus was hailed with derision. He was laughed out of town. This would make most of us despondent. But not Jesus. He took it all in stride. He did not reject his old neighbors. He hailed their reaction as typically human. "A prophet is not without honor, except in his own country, and among his own kin, and in his own house," he said (6:4). He "marveled because of their unbelief" (6:6), but he wasn't threatened by their rejection. His confidence was such that he saw it as their problem, not his.

'He Was Not Following Us'

Jesus was so secure in his mission he was not even bothered by those doing the same work—a notable contrast with many of our fellow workers. Various persons we know are insecure with their commitments, their accomplishments, their routine tasks. They are therefore threatened by the accomplishments of others and see them as competition to be defeated. Even Jesus' disciples came to him with the report that a man was going about casting out demons and had the audacity to do it in Jesus' name (9:38). The disciples were jealous for Jesus and demanded that the man stop because he did not belong to their group. Jesus did not know anything about the man as far as we can tell. But he exhibited no jealousy. He didn't call the disciples together for a strategy meeting on how to stop him.

He didn't seem worried that the man might accelerate in influence and win adherents. In fact, he said, "Do not forbid him; for no one who does a mighty work in my name will be able soon after to speak evil of me" (9:39).

Jesus faced many dangers, but he was confident that however severe, they were not final, even if fatal. The disciples were rowing across the sea of Galilee in the middle of the night. A severe storm arose, and they became fearful. Jesus, sensing their plight, walked on the sea toward them. He called out to them in a calm, reassuring voice. "Take heart, it is I; have no fear. And he got into the boat with them and the wind ceased" (6:50-51).

They Were Amazed

The ultimate in confidence however, was exhibited by Jesus as he made his way toward Jerusalem. He himself anticipated impending doom. The disciples were jittery. They did not know what to expect, and anticipated the worst. "and they were on the road going up to Jerusalem, and Jesus was walking ahead of them; and they were amazed, and those who followed were afraid" (10:32). But Jesus moved ahead unruffled. He knew who he was. He knew where he was going, and why he was going.

> And taking the twelve again, he began to tell them what was going to happen to him, saying, "Behold, we are going up to Jerusalem; and the Son of man will be delivered to the chief priests and the scribes, and they will condemn him to death."
>
> Mark 10:32-33

Jesus had no illusions about this trip. He embraced these developments as indicative of God's purposes. The reasons so many of us approach the tasks of life with so many questions and are discouraged much of the time is that we don't really know who we are or where we are going. For that reason we are justified in being despondent.

Jesus knew that death was in the making, but he vas fearless (10:33). At Jerusalem he cast the money changers out of the temple. The chief priests and their coherts were amazed at his audacity. They asked him by what authority he did these things. Jesus knew he had the truth of God. But he also knew that unless he called on heavenly forces he was defenseless. He knew that his opponents held life and death in their hands. But he was dauntless. He spoke right back. "Was the baptism of John from heaven or from man? Answer me" (11:30). Those looking on knew that the question was too hot to handle, so they refused to answer. They knew of John's popularity. Jesus, knowing that momentarily they had been put in their place, responded, "Neither will I tell you by what authority I do these things" (11:33).

'So That Pilate Wondered'

Even in the face of death, Jesus proceeded with that same air of certitude. He spent the night before the catastrophic last day praying and struggling in the garden. The disciples slept. Jesus struggled in great anguish for several hours trying to reconcile the end with his own desire to live. Finally he was resigned to the inevitable. "It is enough, the hour has come; the Son of man is betrayed into the hands of sinners. Rise, let us be going; see, my betrayer is at hand" (14:41-42). He was apprehended as a criminal and taken before the magistrates. But even as he stood before the high priest (14:61), and before the Roman governor Pilate, the final authority, he sustained the same confidence. "And Pilate asked him, 'Are you the king of the Jews?' And he answered him, 'You have said so' . . . but Jesus made no further answer, so that Pilate wondered" (15:2, 5). Jesus was neither snivelly nor blubbery as he faced death. He was calm, confident, courageous. Indeed, his death was a human death. He struggled with all the great questions, the loneliness, the uncertainty, the estrangement, the nothingness, the compelling desire to live. But once resolved, he accepted it as it arrived, despite the many fruitful remaining years which might otherwise have been his prospect.

'Do Not Be Anxious'

Jesus by design offered his own life as a model for the disciples. He expected them to exhibit the same confidence. When he first sent them out on their own, "He charged them to take nothing for their journey except a staff; no bread, no bag, no money in their belts; but to wear sandals and not put on two tunics" (6:8). He expected occasional rejection. But they were not to be vindictive nor frightened nor despondent. They were to let those who refused know that other opportunities awaited. "If any place will not receive you and they refuse to hear you, when you leave, shake off the dust that is on your feet for a testimony against them" (6:11).

Near the end Jesus prepared the disciples by forewarning them that they would bear testimony before governors and kings. They were to do so with the same calmness and confidence that characterized Jesus. They could do this, not on their own, but through his Spirit who supplied the confidence.

> And when they bring you to trial and deliver you up, do not be anxious beforehand what you are to say; but say whatever is given you in that hour, for it is not you who speak, but the Holy Spirit.

Mark 13:11

When the disciples later ascertained where it was all going, they, too, would be sure of who they were, where they were going, and why.

Exuding Confidence

We are far removed from the days of Jesus. We did not personally see him heal the terrible man in the tombs. We did not hear him speak to the Pharisees when they accused him of receiving power from the Prince of demons. We did not walk with him as he fearlessly approached Jerusalem. But he expects the same confidence from us as he did from those first disciples. He is likewise with us. He has revealed to us who we are, that is, sons of God. He has shown us where we are going, that is, to the place with God which he has prepared. He invites us to locate ourselves, to find our identity, not through rigorous scrutiny of our inner psyche and emotion, but through hearing of the story of the Son.

He expects that we be confident first of all because we will receive from God whatever we ask—that is, if it contributes to the welfare of God's creatures. He expects us to have the self-confidence to leave when asked by those who don't care to hear us anymore. Just as Jesus, we aren't expected to make them like it, regardless. He expects us to accept "no," to face rejection without becoming hysterical or neurotic. He expects us to stand before our superiors, however important, with the calm confidence of God's presence.

Impossible, you say! Of course—if one has to rely on his own ingenuity, be left to his own devices, and generate his own resources. But look at Jesus. Let him be the model. Accept the power he extends. Let him be your confidence!

...to Be
FORCEFUL 11

In our time when life-style is problematic, all types of people are searching for authority figures. A few years ago Gurus dominated the news. Every talk show managed to interview one or more. The appeal of *The Godfather* was that he took charge. *Star Wars* was successful at the box office because when Luke Skywalker opposed gigantic powers of evil, he won. We want a man who, when he speaks something happens. We want a person who has real authority. It is for this reason that Jesus was noticed. The forcefulness of his life was not missed by movie makers in *Jesus Christ Superstar* and *Godspell*.

Jesus came across as a person of authority. This was his appeal to the Romans. Mark was aware of the breakdown of old Roman ways. He said to the Romans, "Here is one who knows what he is about. He comes on with authority. Roman life-styles are folding, but Jesus shows the way to a new and better life." The story of Jesus as told today often makes the same impression.

He Taught Them With Authority

It is sometimes thought that if a person makes no effort to call attention to himself he will end up nondescript and ignored. Some think that without advance publicity they will fade into the crowd and be lost. Churches frequently suppose that the way to cut a swath in their community is to dream up creative means of splashing themselves across the advertising media. How can one make an impression? How can he have authority unless he tells his own story?

The life of Jesus contradicts such thinking. In discussing the unassuming nature of Jesus (chapter 2) we noticed that not only did Jesus forego setting up a public relations committee, he tried to inhibit publicity created by others. Despite Jesus' efforts to go unheralded, news about him spread like wildfire in the hillside villages and along the sea. With our manner of looking at things we are in a quandary. Why did Jesus make the front page when he tried his best to keep out of the paper altogether? What happened simply seems to defy the ground rules of life. Mark has an answer. Jesus made the headlines, not because he planned or intended to do so, but because the power of his words and action captivated those who saw and heard. Jesus' contempories had heard many things, but much of it was bland. They were bombarded, as we are, with words from all sides. Much of the time they slept through because nothing much ever happened. But when Jesus spoke there were results. He taught as one having authority. He captured the imagination. He didn't have to manufacture public relations. He was for real, and the word got out!

One can obviously read the Jesus story from a number of perspectives. He can hail Jesus as a great moral leader. He can see him as a charlatan. He can even confess him as God! But regardless of the presuppositions with which the story is read, one must admit that Jesus impressed people. He was noticed by both friend and foe. He commanded attention. He was remembered for the stark authoritativeness of his presence. We would know nothing about him now if such were not the case.

The first time Jesus set out to teach he was in a synagogue in Capernaum. The response was electrifying. "And they were astonished at his teaching, for he taught them as one who had authority, and not as the scribes" (1:22). Why did Jesus' teaching create such astonishment? What was there about it which made it stand out?

First of all, it seems unlikely the difference was in what Jesus taught. John preached "a baptism for repentance for the forgiveness of sins" (1:4). Jesus likewise from the beginning proclaimed "The time is fulfilled, and the kingdom of God is at hand; repent, and believe in the gospel" (1:15). In terms of content there is little difference in the two messages. But those who accompanied Jesus and watched him saw a difference. They became aware of an authority in Jesus which John did not possess. Mark, strangely enough, in view of his emphasizing Jesus as the Teacher, does not tell what Jesus said at Capernaum. Perhaps he means us to assume that the message was that stated earlier

(1:15). What was said apparently wasn't Mark's focus.

It could be that the manner in which Jesus spoke impressed his hearers. He may have orated with a clear and booming voice. His enunciation may have been precise. He may have spoken with great force and emotion. He may have commanded with such determination and definiteness that people sat up and listened with rapt attention. He may have punctuated each point with forceful gestures. But Mark does not say so.

It may be, too, that Jesus spoke as if the force of his statements resided in himself alone. The scribes usually cited the Old Testament and its various rabbinic interpreters to emphasize their authority. Their authority thus resided in others, not in themselves. It may well be that, from the first, people noticed that Jesus did not depend on the judgments of esteemed rabbis, but presumed that what he said stood on its own intrinsic merits or his personal authority. At least in all the reports about Jesus he never cited rabbinic interpretations to prove his point. Although Palestinians may have noticed this difference, this was obviously not Mark's point. He was addressing Romans, and a Roman gentile would not know that scribes quoted the rabbis.

Mark did not hesitate to offer explanations when he felt his readers needed them. An example is the statement about the hand-washing custom of the Jews.

> Now when the Pharisees gathered together to him, with some of the scribes, who had come from Jerusalem, they saw that some of his disciples ate with hands defiled, that is un-

washed. (For the Pharisees, and all the Jews, do not eat unless they wash their hands, observing the tradition of the elders; and when they come from the market place, they do not eat unless they purify themselves; and there are many other traditions which they observe, the washing of cups and pots and vessles of bronze.)

Mark 7:1-4

If Mark had wished to make the point that the method of Jesus' teaching differed he would have explained the rabbinic approach. Apparently he was not at all interested in the fact that scribes quoted rabbinic predecessors.

It may have likewise been that Jesus' hearers recognized in his speaking a manner different from the prohets of earlier times. When the prophets spoke they often prefaced their remarks with "Thus says the Lord." Jesus never did that. Some of Jesus' contemporaries may have noticed this absence, but if so Mark has no interest in it.

It may be, too, that by his authority the crowds saw in Jesus the power of legislation. They may have envisioned, when he spoke that the very law of God was being delivered. But Mark does not present Jesus as delivering a new law from God.

'And They Obey Him'

So all the answers suggested thus far have failed. We could, no doubt, come up with still others. But what did Mark have in mind when he reported that Jesus' hearers were struck by his authority? If one limits his conclusion to the text of Mark itself the answer is clear. The authority of Jesus is that when he spoke *things happened*. After stating that Jesus

142

impressed people with his authority, Mark reported, "And immediately there was in their synagogue a man with an unclean spirit; and he cried out, 'What have you to do with us, Jesus of Nazareth!' " Uncanny powers were unleashed when Jesus spoke. Through further speaking Jesus controlled these powers. Jesus commanded the unclean spirit, "Be silent, and come out of him!" (1:25). At Jesus' words "The unclean spirit, convulsing him and crying with a loud voice, came out of him." Those present were amazed at the result.

> And they were all amazed, so that they questioned among themselves, saying, "What is this? A new teaching! With authority he commands even the unclean spirits, and they obey him."
>
> Mark 1:27

Notice the "new teaching" was not so much what Jesus said but what happened when he said it. Mark did not report any long speeches of Jesus. He did not include many parables. It was not so much what Jesus said but what *happened* when he said it that impressed Mark. Results impressed Mark, and it was this that he had in mind when he spoke of the authority of Jesus.

"...the 'new teaching' was not so much what Jesus said, but what happened when he said it."

In chapter 2, Mark tells the story of the paralytic who was let down on a pallet through an opening in the roof. Jesus said to the paralytic "My son, your sins are forgiven" (2:5). Certain scribes sitting on the sidelines were quick to charge blasphemy. "Who can forgive sins but God alone?" No prophet ever took upon himself the power to forgive sin. Prophets did pray to God on man's behalf and solicited God's forgiveness. About Abraham it was said, "for he is a prophet, and will pray for you, and you shall live" (Gen. 20:7). Prophets often interceded for people, making specific requests of God. Sometimes their prayers were granted; sometimes not. In one situation Jeremiah prayed at length, and with great fervor, but God rejected the petition. But even in refusal is the recognition that God often heard the pleas of the prophets and fulfilled their request. " 'Though Moses and Samuel stood before me, yet my heart would not turn toward this people. Send them out of my sight, and let them go!' " (Jer. 15:1-2).

Jesus claimed unusual prerogatives. He did not petition God to forgive the paralytic's sins. He *commanded* forgiveness as if he himself had that ability. His power was not derived. It was his own. He had authority in his own being. But his authority resided not in crass, fiat pronouncements. His authority was authenticated by what resulted from his speaking.

> "But that you may know that the son of man has authority on earth to forgive sins—he said to the paralytic—"I say to you, rise take up your pallet and go home." And he rose, and immediately took up the pallet and went out before them all; so that they were all amazed and glorified God, saying, "We never saw anything like this."
>
> Mark 2:10-12

144

Jesus' authority was demonstrated by the fact that when he told the paralytic to walk, he walked!

When He Spoke Things Happened

People sat up and noticed when Jesus talked. He spoke with amazing authority. When most people talk little happens. It is like someone speaking into a dead microphone. But when Jesus spoke there was a "happening!" In effect, Mark said to the Romans, "If you wish to identify with someone who has power and authority, follow Jesus!"

That Mark wishes to identify the authority of Jesus with what happened when he spoke is clear from the number of places in which Mark calls Jesus "Teacher," or speaks of his teaching, and tells nothing of the teaching content. We are surprised in various instances that Mark's favorite title for Jesus is Teacher. What he tells us about the activities of Jesus does not at all lead us to expect that designation. We have already noticed the Capernaum synagogue incident (1:21-22). Jesus was again identified as Teacher during a storm on the sea. The disciples were fearful for their lives and cried out "Teacher, do you not care if we perish?" (4:38).

Then again, the ruler came to solicit Jesus' aid in behalf of his daughter. Upon hearing that the daughter had just died, the man's friends said to him, "Why trouble the Teacher any further?" (5:35). So often when Jesus was called the Teacher he did not launch into a lengthy discussion but instead performed a mighty work (see also 9:17, 38). In fact, in some cases Jesus is called Teacher in the Greek (for example 11:21) and the translator translated it "master." Mark obviously connected the role of Jesus as Teacher with the action which follows upon Jesus' speaking. His authority resided in the fact that when he spoke, something happened!

Authoritative Living Now

Now, 1,900 years later, Mark still says "No one ever spoke like this man." Why follow a Guru? Why immortalize political heroes such as Barry Goldwater, George McGovern, or Jimmy Carter? All these men have feet of clay. Why expend so much energy to elevate or worship Elvis Presley, John Denver, or Olivia Newton-John? All these people fade with the years. But where Jesus is, there is power. Where he is, things happen. Where he is, things get done. Jesus has authority.

So what does all this mean, you say? So I accept him. So I follow him. So I find him authoritative. What does his authority say for my life-style? He had authority because he was Son of God! I can't have authority of this kind. But perhaps that conclusion is too hasty. Jesus did not retain his authority for himself.

First, Jesus conferred that same authority on the twelve. Their life, therefore, was also one of authority. Mark tells how Jesus took the twelve aside and transferred to them the ability to speak so as to make things happen.

> And he went up into the hills, and called to him those whom he desired; and they came to him. And he appointed twelve, to be with him, and to send out to preach, and have authority to cast out demons.
>
> Mark 3:13-15

Jesus did not selfishly reserve his powers for him-

146

self. He shared with the twelve his abilities so that the very foundations of demonic power were shaken. Later, when Jesus sent the twelve out two by two, this conferred authority became obvious. "And he called to him the twelve, and began to send them out two by two and gave them authority over the unclean spirits" (6:7). This power was derived from Jesus himself. Mark said very little about the Holy Spirit. There is the sense in the New Testament that the Spirit is the Spirit of Jesus (Phil. 1:19); that he is sent in the name of Jesus (John 14:26); and in fact is identical with Jesus (2 Cor. 3:17).

But power for the disciples also comes from the Holy Spirit:

> And when they bring you to trial and deliver you up, do not be anxious beforehand what you are to say; but say whatever is given you in that hour, for it is not you who speak, but the Holy Spirit.

Mark 13:11

Jesus himself will continue his work among those who affirm him even from his position in heaven at the right hand of God. "And they went forth and preached everywhere, while the Lord worked with them and confirmed the message by the signs that attended it" (16:20).

"All right," we may say. "Jesus lived authoritatively, and he gave authority to his disciples, too. But what does this have to do with me? It is not clear that demonic powers are about us today, despite *The Exorcist*. Even if they are, I doubt very much that I can have power over them." Perhaps not. But we are surrounded by dark forces which in many regards are as inexplicable as these ancient ones. It is striking that those who trust Jesus, who pray to him for wisdom, who stand in the presence of dark forces, even now discover that their words have authority. Even now, those who follow Jesus speak, and things happen!

His Authority Expressed Through Us

A college student was weighed down with many problems. She was not good looking. She was overweight. She had no boyfriend. She didn't like school. She was on the verge of failing her courses. She was having battles with her parents. She had no friends. One night she decided to end it all by taking an overdose of sleeping pills. Fortunately, she was discovered the next morning before the pills had their lethal effect. A girl with a deep commitment to Jesus, who had been studying his life, saw the crisis and stepped in. She talked with the girl at length. She prayed with her. She let her know she cared. Her words had authority. Things happened. The would-be suicide developed a new outlook on life. She returned to school. She ironed out some of the conflicts with her parents. She even acquired a boyfriend. Was the power of the friend's words because of the authority of Jesus?

A thiry-year-old Canadian woman in the Boston area had various mental problems and had spent considerable money on psychiatrists. For a time she was in a state mental hospital, lapsing into the twilight zone again. Her psychiatrist refused to see her. Her husband, out of concern, talked with their preacher. He asked if he could counsel with her if she became overly distraught. The minister said yes but felt very inadequate. How could he step in and do anything when the psychiatrists had failed?

He called her psychiatrist. The psychiatrist volunteered very little. He said to go ahead and work with her, it would do no harm. What authority could a mere preacher have over such a debilitating, perplexing illness?

"When words are spoken with faith in Jesus...the unexpected occurs, and the authoritative life-style of Jesus is reproduced."

Late one night the husband called the minister. His wife was worse, and he asked the minister to come. The minister didn't know what he could do. But he went, saying a prayer on the way, asking for wisdom, trusting he would say the right thing. He decided not to talk, but to listen. The right words might emerge later. The three sat in darkness for a time. Little was said. The woman talked occasionally. She said she felt like a rubber band wound up so tight it was about to break. After awhile the minister asked is she liked living in the Boston area. She said she did not, that she would really like to go back to Deer Island, Canada, where they had formerly lived. After a minute or so the husband spoke up. "I didn't know you felt that way. If you really want to, we will move back." Another period of silence followed. The wife said, "I would like that!" She then said she felt better and would like to go to sleep.

In two weeks, in a way that at least amazed the preacher, the woman's mental illness had almost completely disappeared. She was excited about plans for returning to Deer Island. The preacher had trusted Jesus and his Father. He knew he had no power. But behind his words was the authority of Jesus. As they were spoken, something happened.

The authority of Jesus is even now a possible life-style for the one who trusts him. Where the story of Jesus is known and received into a life, there authority is to be found. If one shuns the headlines, if he places himself in the hands of the Teacher as servant, Jesus supplies authority to his words. The opposing forces may be indifferent, uncanny, inexplicable. But when words are spoken with faith in Jesus and because of him, the unexpected occurs, and the authoritative life-style of Jesus is reproduced.

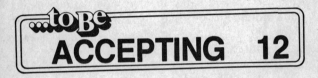

...to Be
ACCEPTING 12

Death is the persistent tragedy of these times. Few other problems remain so far beyond the reach of human effort and ingenuity. True, there are dark and dangerous features of contemporary existence which we have not conquered. We have not rid the world of heart disease, cancer, smog, water pollution, energy depletion, war, discrimination, starvation, and ignorance. But at least we have worked diligently and systematically on these problems and have attained considerable insight into them. In some cases we have attacked the causes of such problems so successfully that victory has been complete. Smallpox and polio have essentially disappeared. We have learned how to control venereal diseases, flu epidemics, measles, and many other diseases (though obviously people do not always avail themselves of cures). We have cut down on smog and river pollution. It seems that we have the know-how and the technology to

151

take care of most of the problems of the universe, given time and money.

Facing Death

But one problem remains, namely, death. In recent years, death has also been studied scientifically. For legal purposes, definitions of death have been hammered out from precise physiological indicators. Even more energy has gone into the study of the psychic stages of dying persons. It is true that considerably more is now known about the unfolding moods and psychological suffering of those about to die. From observations and discussions with the dying, some have even presumed to speak of what lies beyond death.

But despite all these new investigations, death remains a mystery. We can have little confidence that scientists and psychologists, given time, will really discover what death is all about and develop means to overcome it. Death remains the one mysterious and unconquerable fact for man, which he has no hope of changing.

Modern discoveries, increasing the length of life, have made death even more tragic. Death's time, with care, is postponed, making escape seem possible. But despite careful precautions, death is not ultimately side-stepped. We have prolonged life by listening to a continuous stream of message. We have had our yearly check-ups for cancer and high blood pressure. We have fastened our seat belts. We have stopped smoking, and gone on numerous diets. We have supported peace efforts to end the slaughter of our young men and women. Through these means we have prolonged life. But eventually death catches up with us. It comes as a horrendous blow because to date we have seemed so successful in warding it off. We have spent so much time avoiding death and have had so little contact with it that when it finally arrives we are totally unprepared. This is so, whether the death is ours or that of another.

"...Just as we are to follow Jesus in the manner in which he lived, we are to follow him in the manner in which he faced death."

Jesus' life included a manner of facing death. Mark commended the style of Jesus, not only in the way he lived, but also in the way he died. The life of Jesus in this respect had a special message for Christians living in Rome in the latter part of the first century. Unlike us, they regularly faced the hard realities of death. Christians even took on a new burden, for they were frequently called upon to confess the deity of the Roman emperor, or else die for confessing Jesus as Lord. Although modern Christians are rarely asked to die for our faith, we still face death, and the way Jesus confronted this terminal time still speaks even to us.

Apparently, the common view among Christians and others who have heard Christian preaching is that Christians face death in hope, faith, and expectancy. Christians who find themselves fearful and resentful sometimes reprove themselves for those feelings and conclude that they are persons of little faith. Thus, they speak to each other of the death of a loved one they often encourage a negation of sorrow and despair. They speak of the loved one being with God. They speak of the hope of the resurrection. They speak as if tears and terror are out of place for the Christian. Somehow, these are sub-Christian modes of behavior.

Before forming hasty conclusions one way or the other, it would be well to study the manner in which Jesus faced death. We might here suggest that just as we are to follow Jesus in the manner in which he lived, we are to follow him in the manner in which he faced death.

'The Son Of Man Must Suffer'

Included in Jesus' plans for life were plans for death. He affirmed that God gives life and likewise takes it away. An individual does not control when he is born nor when he dies. Death is not merely the culmination of natural aging processes. It is a divine decision and determined by God according to his purposes for those who turn their life over to him. Of course, there is that part of creation which makes up its own rules and goes its own way. It stands opposed to God. God relates to that part of creation in a different manner.

"He expected to usher in the rule of God, not by sitting in a palatial throne room in Jerusalem, but through death!"

Jesus differed from other persons in that he knew the circumstances and rapidly-approaching time of his death. But his death was, as much as his life, an event in the purposes of God. In that regard it was like the death of all persons who turn their lives over to God. The conclusion that God oversees even death is expressed a number of places in the Scriptures (for example, Ps. 104:29 and Phil. 1:19-20).

Mark tells of three times when Jesus forewarned his disciples of his impending death. In each case he accepted death along with its purposes. The first occasion is shortly after the disciples confess the astounding conviction that Jesus is the Christ. This realization had come slowly. At first, like others, they apparently considered Jesus a prophet. But they knew that for centuries prophets had spoken of God sending relief in a time in which his people were greatly afflicted. Relief would be brought by a servant whom God would raise up. He would be anointed to perform God's tasks. The disciples, along with others, both learned and unlearned, apparently expected this servant to be anointed as king. He would rule in Palestine in the manner of David, Solomon, and Hezekiah. As the disciples observed Jesus they became increasingly impressed with his extraordinary powers. No prophet was able to accomplish his mighty works. He cast out demons, he fed the hungry, he healed the sick, he spoke to storms and they were calmed. A man with those powers could overthrow Roman tyranny and restore the rule of God to Palestine as in the ancient empire. So many of Jesus' followers anticipated a glorious future for him. They confessed him as the king expected by the great prophets. But they were almost totally unprepared for Jesus' future as he himself envisioned it. His understanding was almost exactly opposite from theirs. He expected to usher in the rule of God, not by sitting in a palatial throne room in Jerusalem, but through *death!* As he saw it, God gave him life for that very reason.

And he began to teach them that the Son of man must suffer many things, and be rejected by the elders and the chief priests and the scribes, and be killed, and after three days rise again.

Mark 8:31

Peter simply could not believe his ears. Jesus spoke with such plainness the disciples couldn't miss the point. But they did not understand, since it was so opposed to their fondest hopes for Jesus. How can death be the beginning of a kingly rule? So Peter rebuked Jesus. But Jesus stopped him, then spoke back: "Get behind me, Satan! You are not on the side of God, but of man" (8:33). To Peter and others it simply did not make sense that one with so many godly talents could be taken by God so young. Furthermore he would miss any chance to restore Israel to her former grandeur.

'They Did Not Understand'

The affirmation of Jesus concerning his death was so foreign to the disciples that he felt compelled to teach them about it. They could not fathom a suffering messiah. But Jesus explained it to them in words indelibly etched on their minds even though they did not believe them at the time.

"The Son of man will be delivered into the hands of men, and they will kill him; and when he is killed, after three days he will rise." But they did not understand the saying, and they were afraid to ask him.

Mark 9:31-32

Jesus accepted his early death not as an accident but as the will of God. He did not conceive it as merely a human conspiracy or the grinding wheels of political expediency, even though such was involved. He understood death as the fruition of his work on behalf of men. His death as well as his life spoke of who he was. Death was threatening but not absurd or without meaning. It had purpose in itself. And beyond death was resurrection and opportunity to enjoy life with God forever. Death means the completion of an earthly task in order to go on to others of greater consequence.

"Death means the completion of an earthly task in order to go on to others of greater consequence."

But still the disciples did not understand. James and John came to Jesus and requested to sit on his left and right in his kingdom—that is to be his lieutenants. They still envisioned Jesus as a new David. Jesus again emphasized that his rule would come about through suffering and death. He told them they had much yet to learn. "You do not know what you are asking. Are you able to drink the cup that I drink?" (10:38). By "the cup" he had in mind his death, as is apparent by looking at Mark 14:36, "Remove this cup from me." It was a cup which Jesus did not himself design. They, too, would know that cup, he declared, for God would use their death purposefully. They would serve their fellows just as he had served. Then he suggested that his life and his death spoke one message: the way of God is the way of service. "For the Son of man also came not to be served but to serve, and to give his life as a ransom for many" (10:45).

The purpose of the death of Jesus was to release men and women enslaved by sin. The rule of God which Jesus ushered in was inexhaustible. The implications were more far reaching than the disciples envisioned. It was a release from the kingdom of darkness, an entry into the kingdom of light. That citizenship became available to all men regardless of nationality, race, or creed. Later they learned.

'Remove This Cup From Me'

Jesus accepted his death from God. But he did not accept it passively, without a fight. If Jesus shows the way of life as well as the way of death, he indicates that God does not necessarily intend that man accept his end calmly and passively. God has always shown himself ready to hear and discuss the outcome of human desires. God determined to destroy Israel when they worshiped the golden calf. But Moses argued on their behalf:

> But Moses besought the Lord his God, and said, "O Lord, why does thy wrath burn hot against thy people, whom thou hast brought forth out of the land of Egypt with great power and with a mighty hand? Why should the Egyptians say, 'With evil intent did he bring them forth, to slay them in the mountains, and to consume them from the face of the earth'? "

Exodus. 32:11-12

God heard and was persuaded. "And the Lord repented of the evil which he thought to do to his people" (32:14).

The Psalmists were never reticent about speaking openly with God about illness, suffering, and

158

anticipated death. Psalm 55, identified as a "Maskill" of David, is straightforward in its plea:

Give ear to my prayer, O God;
   and hide not thyself from my supplication!
Attend to me, and answer me;
   I am overcome by my trouble.
I am distraught by the noise of the enemy,
   because of the oppression of the wicked
For they bring trouble upon me,
   and in anger they cherish enmity against
   me.
My heart is in anguish within me
   the terrors of death have fallen upon me.
Fear and trembling come upon me,
   and horror overwhelms me.

Psalms 55:1-5

But I call upon God;
   and the Lord will save me,
Evening and morning and at noon
   I utter my complaint and moan,
and he will hear my voice.
   He will deliver my soul in safety
from the battle that I wage,
   For many are arrayed against me.

Psalms 55:16-18

The Psalmist believed that in discourse with God, decisions were made and directions changed. In the famous Psalm 22 quoted by Jesus on the cross, the Psalmist openly approached God in full confidence that he would hear and act.

My God, my God, why has thou forsaken
me?
   Why art thou so far from helping me, from
the words of my groaning?

O my God, I cry by day, but thou dost not answer;

    and by night, but find no rest.

Psalm 22:1-2

The Psalmist concludes by praising God for affirmative response and benefits not only for his generation, but future generations: "and proclaim his deliverance to a people yet unborn, that he has wrought it." (22:31)

His Death For Us

Jesus announced his death to the disciples to prepare them for it. He knew it was coming. He knew how and when. He accepted it as the will of God. Yet as the moment approached he grew apprehensive. His fears surfaced. He struggled with himself, and with God. He did not escape the terrors by assuring himself he was the Son of God. He did not take comfort because, as Plato would put it, he had within himself an immortal, indestructible soul. His anxiety apparently was not allayed because he believed and pointedly told the disciples that following his death he would be raised again in three days. Despite whatever hopes he may have entertained as to what awaited beyond, as he approached death he grew more and more fearful. He did not apologize for his behavior. He did not try to hide it. In fact, he hoped the disciples would suffer with him in those moments of despair. He wanted them to know his fear and share it.

The night before his crucifixion Jesus suffered the terror and abandonment of death. He went with his disciples to a place called Gethsemane. He pointed out a certain location to the disciples and told all of them except Peter, James, and John to sit there and pray. He took these three and proceeded farther into the garden (14:33). The thought of death began to strike home. "My soul is very sorrowful, even to death; remain here, and watch." He became so distraught he fell on the ground and prayed and pleaded with God. "Father, all things are possible to thee; remove this cup from me; yet not what I will, but what thou wilt" (14:36). Jesus knew God was approachable even in regard to death. He knew God gives death as well as life. He was willing to accept God's decision for him to die. But he desired otherwise. He did not think pleading with God sacrilegious. He did not think fear of death as being sub-Christian. His death indicated what life was all about. It gave a final interpretation to the hiddenness, suffering, and poverty of existence. After some time in struggle, his desire for life always before him, he accepted the verdict of God. "It is enough: the hour has come; the Son of man is betrayed into the hands of sinners. Rise, let us be going; see, my betrayer is at hand." When God's intentions became clear, Jesus acquiesced. Until then he considered the time of death, as did the Psalmists, negotiable with God.

"He did not think of death as being sub-Christian."

Early the next morning Jesus was taken before Pilate, the Roman governor. Pilate hoped to free Jesus by clearing up the charges against him. But Jesus failed to respond, hence provided no occasion for release. When talking with Jesus failed, Pilate next tried to persuade the people to approve Jesus' release. But they were not so disposed. Pilate thereupon decided he had no altervative but to consign Jesus for crucifixion. The standard procedures followed.

"The terror of his death shows in a profound manner that it was a death of a human like you and me."

Jesus was taken to Golgotha and nailed to a wooden cross. After a few hours he was emaciated in the sun and heat. Finally about noon it grew dark (15:33). At three in the afternoon the end drew near. Jesus remembered the words of the Psalmist who called to God out of his agony. Because of his misery Jesus uttered the same plaintive words, "My God, my God, why hast thou forsaken me?" In Mark's confession, Jesus was Son of God. Yet even the Son, as he approached death, knew the terror of being separated from God who is himself the source of life. Death advanced steathily. God turned his face. He withdrew his sustaining power. Chaos ensued. The void arrived. Nothingness stared Jesus in the face. In that dark moment Jesus abandoned hope. Those present saw the hopelessness with which Jesus faced death. Jesus, unlike Socrates, did not consider this the supreme moment at which to exhibit bravery, fortitude and faith. He faced death for what it really is, a separation from God. The terror of his death was not, as suggested by some, the fact that he bore upon his shoulders the weight of millions of sinners (though in fact, he "gave his life as a ransom for many.") No New Testament text gives that as the reason for his great suffering. The terror of his death shows in a profound manner that it was a death of a human like you and me. He indeed became like us in all respects, even in death. Therefore his death was efficacious for us. It is our death. He suffered it first and won a great victory over it. In so doing he assures us, not that we will escape death, but that we, too, shall win a great victory in it.

Facing Our Death

The death of Jesus shows us the manner in which we can face it. He first of all showed us life's way, then also showed us death's way. We should accept death as a gift from God. It is the end, the completion of a task. We do not decide the time of death nor its place. But if we have turned our life, our calendar, over to God, we believe that death is not purely an accident. Through death God accomplishes his ends.

Second, we should anticipate death before the event as climaxing the meaning of life. If our life is a confession of Jesus, we should confess even unto death. If our life is devoted to service our final moments should be found in service. That was the case with the one whose life we are following. If our life is devoted to giving, we should arrange to give even in death. If we have dedicated our life to teaching then death itself should provide the ultimate occasion for teaching.

Third, God is open to our wrestling with him over death as with other matters. Just as Jesus sought deliverance, so should that be our desire—

we, too, have the prerogative of requesting deliverance. But we must be prepared to accept God's verdict just as did Jesus.

"Jesus was not ashamed of his anxiety in those final moments. Neither should we be ashamed."

Fourth, even though we have before us the hope of resurrection, even as Jesus, we should not reproach ourselves if we are frightened. Jesus did not guard his disciples from his fears. He did not hold that expressing fear is the sign of a lack of faith. Jesus was not ashamed of his anxiety in those final moments. Neither should we be ashamed. We need not blindly accept the commonly held notion that persons of faith should approach death passively, with no feeling one way or the other. Jesus feared death without shame; he frees us to face death in the same manner. "If any man would come after me, let him deny himself and take up his cross and follow me" (8:34).

VICTORIOUS 13

Our age has grown tired of the ways of the fathers. It ventures forth for new life-styles. It locates models here and there. It may just be that, given the opportunity, our epoch will stumble upon Jesus. Then the future will, in a new and victorious manner, be his.

The life-style of Jesus can radiate upon ours in various ways. It speaks to the center of our life. It speaks to the manner in which we appear. It speaks to the way in which we relate to people. It speaks to the manner in which we react to rules and regulations. It speaks to the way in which we regard our time. It even includes an approach to death. All of this is to say that if we accept the life-way of Jesus we become a new person. It further says that if we share this life with others and they, too, accept him, then we will face a future filled with new persons.

'This Man Was The Son Of God'

The life-style of Jesus is critical not simply because he more than any other man was bold, unassuming, confident, forceful, and compassionate. He did indeed live as a man and died as a man. But he was not an ordinary man. Mark commended him because he was the Son of God. Mark spoke of his story as "The beginning of the gospel of Jesus Christ, the Son of God" (1:1).

People do not always come easily and genuinely to the conviction that Jesus is the Son of God. Mark does not suppose they do. He told the story hoping that, as it unfolded, faith would eventually happen. And it did. A whole ancient civilization came to believe in his Sonship. But it did not happen suddenly or easily.

The disciples themselves only gradually awakened to the fact that walking in their very midst was the Son of God. If we share with them their experience, we, too, can arrive at that faith. There are at least three times when Mark declares that Jesus' actions should have brought understanding and faith on the part of the disciples. Each incident failed. But through Mark's Gospel we learn that initial failure is not disastrous. The longer one is with Jesus, the more of the story he hears, the greater the prospect that faith will occur.

The disciples were crossing the sea in a boat. A great storm arose. Jesus was asleep. Even the rapid rising and falling of the swells did not wake him. The disciples grew more and more alarmed. Finally, they felt compelled to arouse Jesus and relate their fear. Jesus remained unexcited and unhurried. He simply rebuked the wind, "Peace! Be still!" (4:39). The wind stopped. The sea subsided. The disciples "were filled with awe, and said to one another, 'Who then is this, that even wind and sea obey him?' " By what unusual power was Jesus able to perform this mighty feat? Who is it who can simply speak and the storms obey? Unless it was a coincidence (that is, at that exact moment the storm was about to die and Jesus said the words at just the right instance), Jesus must have been drawing on powers from beyond. He must be someone associated with God. When God created the dry land from the waters he spoke and it appeared (Gen. 1:9). Jesus spoke and the same waters obeyed his voice. Who is this? The disciples were filled with awe, but did not get the point. "Who then is this . . . ?"

In a somewhat later episode, Jesus, in the presence of the disciples, fed five thousand men from five loaves and two fish. That very same night the disciples were rowing on the sea with the wind against them. Jesus was not along. But then he came, walking on the sea! They thought he was a ghost and cried out in fright. He spoke, "Take heart, it is I; have no fear" (6:50). When he got into the boat the wind ceased. We don't know if Jesus did this to prove his Sonship. But Mark, or the story as he received it, made this point. The five thousand were fed in the wilderness from no visible resources. Jesus walked on the water. The disciples should have put two and two together. But they did not understand. "And they were utterly astounded, for they did not understand about the loaves, but their hearts were hardened" (6:51-52).

Afterward, Jesus once again faced a hungry crowd, and fed four thousand. This time he made explicit for the disciples the implications of these unusual episodes. He fed the crowds because of his deep concern for their welfare. At the same time he hoped the facts would add up for the disciples. Jesus asked them how many baskets of food were taken up after the five thousand ate. They remembered and answered correctly. He next asked how many were taken up after the four thousand. Then he raised the crucial question, "Do you yet understand?" (8:21). Jesus hoped they would discern the nature of these events, and identify the compassionate hand of God moving through them. God created the universe through his word. He fed his people manna and quail in the wilderness. Jesus also spoke to the physical universe and it obeyed. He fed people in the wilderness with no obvious food supply.

Should one correctly connect these events he would ascertain in the actions of Jesus the power of God. He would even see Jesus as the Son of God. What was the matter with these disciples? Only later did the light dawn. It seems to be Mark's point that one cannot really understand who Jesus is and what he was doing apart from his death and resurrection. The point is reiterated once again that the way to glory is the way of the cross. The glory of God is his love and compassion for the universe which he has created and for man made in his image.

Through these incidents, through this story, we, too, are called to believe that Jesus is the Son of God. The disciples came to that realization. The Romans came to that realization. What was possible for them is likewise possible for us. When we finally come to affirm him as Son we become impressed with the need to make our life-style his life-style. Since he is Son he shows what a genuine, authentic, credible existence is like.

'Go Into All The World'

The message of Mark is that the Gospel can produce faith and be victorious in our world. He remembered the charge of Jesus, "Go into all the world and preach the gospel to the whole creation. He who believes and is baptized will be saved; but he who does not believe will be condemned" (16:15-16).

We stand amazed at the manner in which Jesus entered households in Rome. The city was laden with tradition, but also teeming with newcomers with all sorts of moral values and sometimes almost none at all. We are filled with wonder at the rapidity with which toward the end of the second century Jesus began to bring the Roman capitol under his discipline—bristling, erratic Rome. The Jesus story was first told in Rome in the '30s. By the time Rome burned in A.D. 64, the Christians had become notorious enough that Nero, the emperor, laid the blame at their door. By the time Mark produced his Gospel in the early '70s, Jesus was already being confessed by various segments of Roman society all the way from landed gentry to slaves. The seed planted rapidly took root. The early Christians had taken their Lord seriously when he said to go into all the world and tell the story. Those who worshiped in Jesus' name made up a significant and vocal, though persecuted, minority. The name of Jesus could be heard in suburban households, in the alleys and the main thoroughfares. His name even echoed in whispers from the corridors of the emperor's palace.

The apostle Paul was in some measure responsible for the infiltration of Christianity into the palace circles. In the late '60s he was imprisoned in Rome. But he used the occasion as an opportunity to tell all his soldier guards the Jesus story. He wrote the Philippian Christians, "I want you to know, brethren, that what has happened to me has really served to advance the gospel, so that is has become known throughout the whole praetorian guard" (Phil. 1:12-13). Mark and others presented Jesus, and Jesus won over a civilization. In days of uncertainty and confusion Jesus struck a solid note. Where there was cowardice he commended boldness. Where there was cruelty he spoke of compassion. Where there was indecision he encouraged decisiveness.

It may hardly seem believable that a Jew from far-off Palestine turned upside down such a powerful, sophisticated, yet unruly society. But the Romans were seeking a new way of life. Their old ways had turned sour, and they had turned against the strange and mystical Eastern religions that had been imported. When Jesus arrived upon the scene, a new light dawned. Some 200 years later, Christianity became the official religion of the Empire, a regime which not too many years earlier still operated under the false illusion that it might be possible to eradicate this faith which claimed so much and so many. The Jesus story had power. Society was falling apart. As people looked for new security and meaning they turned to Jesus of Nazareth. He made the same impression on Rome as he had earlier in Palestine.

We live in days which some church historians label "post-Christian." They apparently see a permanent demise of Christianity as an intellectual force in the western world. Christianity, of course, has only attained majority status among western nations. It has never been the major religion of the world. So perhaps the decline of Christianity in the west, especially in Europe, where almost no one goes to church anymore, marks the eclipse of Christianity. But then Jesus has always had his ups and downs in history. Jesus envisioned, in fact, times when Christians would run into trouble:

> And brother will deliver up brother to death, and the father his child, and children will rise against parents and have them put to death; and you will be hated by all for my name's sake.
>
> Mark 13:12-13

"What is required is a new generation of believers. These will be people who have internalized the life-style of Jesus..."

When one has placed his hope in Jesus, despite present setbacks he is not yet ready to give up the faith. He is not unrealistic about the manner in which Jesus is being ignored in various quarters. But he is not about to forfeit the prospect that Jesus can and will indeed make a come back. In fact, even now among the "common people," always Jesus' stronghold, new signs of life are evident. Part of the problem is that the Jesus story has been told in so many different ways and so many traditions have accrued, that the real Jesus has to some extent been lost to twentieth century man. It could be that in order for a new and vibrant Christianity to arise, the encrustations of a Christian civil religion must pass from the scene.

The intellectual trappings of western Christianity are in some measure inimical to the Jesus of the New Testament.

Where the real Jesus stands up, where a Gospel such as that presented by Mark is read and then taken seriously, Jesus returns as excitingly fresh. His life-style, uncluttered by the barnacles of tradition, shines forth in new clarity. He provides the power to live victorious lives. What is required is a new generation of believers. These will be people who have internalized the life-style of Jesus and who are attempting to emulate him vigorously and fully. Where this happens Jesus' star will rise again over the horizon, even in the West. He will once again lead a newly dedicated people in the way of God. The first Christians believed Jesus was the man for their time. They went out, they spoke, and people heard. A whole civilization saw him beckon, and they followed. He will shine in the same manner above our horizon if we take up his cross and follow.

And Jesus Went With Them

Jesus will have the same influence on our civilization he had on Rome if we take up his life-style. This can happen because he continues his work through those who take up his cross and follow him. He does not leave the advance of the kingdom merely to human powers, though it begins as the work of dedicated women and men. He works with and through those servants who have responded to his call. He empowers them to take up the task, and supplies the wherewithal to complete it (16:19-20).

We can do so many things like Jesus. Just as he

172

did not seek the spotlights, so can we. Just as he identified with the humble rather than with the proud and haughty, so can we. But he does not leave us with self-striving operations. He supplies power from on high as we work with and pray for those who are distraught and diseased. He supplies courage and wisdom as we confess who he is to our fellows. He gives us the time to complete his assigned tasks.

"...what we cannot do under our own power he can do through us if we allow him."

G. K. Chesterton once said, "Christianity has not been tried and found wanting. It has been found difficult and not tried." Opposition is always raised by those professing to believe in Jesus, when someone proposes seriously that Jesus should be followed in life-style. One of the main reasons for the decline of Jesus in the West may well be the various rationalizations for withholding commitment to his way of life.

Jesus indicated by what he did and said that his followers should stay out of the limelight. A church leader says, "You can't be serious to propose that we Christians and the church should not advertise. After all, if we don't let the community know we are here, how can we reach anyone? The church has to grow. How is it going to bring people in without publicity? If we won't put on public relations campaigns who will hear about us?" Jesus saw this as hollow reasoning. A church where the love and work of God is manifest cannot be hid. People will hear about it, just as when Jesus pledged people to silence, the word leaked out. A church creates publicity and grows, not by manufacturing artificial attention getters, but by being the church of Jesus Christ.

Another person says, "Well, after all, Jesus was Son of God. He had powers we can never have." That's true. He accomplished extraordinary feats that we can never repeat such as raising the dead and restoring sight to the blind. But all power in heaven and on earth has been given him; and he shares it with us. He provides victories beyond our fondest dreams when we open our lives to him. Oh, what bland and impotent lives we live when we depict him as accomplishing all and we ourselves as powerless! Of course we can accomplish nothing for him by ourselves! But what we cannot do under our own power he can do through us if we allow him.

Another person says, "Jesus lived in a different age. Our life is so much different. We have to live by a clock. We cannot take seriously his haphazard approach to time. Why, we'd never get anything done." So we throw up all these smoke screens and sit back engulfed by the fog. The world finds its own saviors while we withhold our very being from the real Lord. They certainly have no chance to see him through us. We sit around speaking of the person who takes Jesus seriously as having soft spots on the brain and being some sort of a mystic.

Taking Mark Seriously

So the life-style of Jesus is observed like the treasures of Egypt from the tomb of King Tut. It is admired but not emulated. It is held up as an ideal for another world, another time, but not for this age. Mark meant business when he presented Jesus to the Romans of his day. He was not just telling a good story. He was not interested in another literary masterpiece after the manner of the great Roman Virgil, in his epic poem *The Aeneid*. He was not satisfied if his work was simply read and admired. He was asking men and women to emulate the very life Jesus lived. Many took Mark seriously. The result was that Jesus commandeered a people wandering about listlessly, not knowing in what direction they headed. They were like sheep without a shepherd.

And many in our time don't know where to turn for leadership. Our political leaders have all turned out to have feet of clay. Religious leaders many times seem more interested in prominence and financial security than service. In our times, as Mark's people are searching. We need to take up the Jesus story once again in its starkness and boldness. It will preach! It will live! Jesus is the leader our time is searching for. The name of Jesus will be heard again in our corridors and on our roadways. He still beckons, and where he is embraced, the kingdom of God follows. If this is a post-Christian era, it is not that he wills it, but we will it.

'Follow Me!'

Where Jesus is embraced, the kingdom of God grows. To take him seriously is to follow him as he is, as he is presented by those who know him. To follow the reinterpretations, qualifications, and rationalizations of later compromises is not to take him seriously. The real Jesus can spring up

175

through the ashes of a post-Christian era. The parable of the mustard seed apparently does not envision a once-for-all growth with no decline or death. Rather, it affirms that whenever Jesus enters a life, a seed, however small, is sown. From that small beginning enormous growth occurs.

> With what can we compare the kingdom of God, or what parable shall we use for it? It is like a grain of mustard seed, which, when sown upon the ground, is the smallest of all the seeds on earth; yet when it is sown it grows up and becomes the greatest of all shrubs, and puts forth large branches, so that the birds of the air can make nests in its shade.

Mark 4:30-32

In the words of Phillips Brooks' immortal "Oh Little Town of Bethlehem,"

> No ear may hear His coming;
>   But in this world of sin,
> Where meek souls will receive Him still,
>   the dear Christ enters in.

When that happens it is because men and women, young people and old, commit themselves to the life-style of Jesus as a way to live. They turn from themselves to others in compassion and helpfulness just as Jesus spent his life for others. And still he calls:

> If any man would come after me, let him deny himself and take up his cross and follow me. For whoever would save his life will lose it; and whoever loses his life for my sake and the gospel's will save it.

Mark 8:34-35